TOWN AND TOWNSCAPE

BY THE SAME AUTHOR

Town and Countryside
English Panorama
Town Planning
The Anatomy of the Village
Oxford Replanned
Cathedral City
Exeter Phoenix
Georgian City
Newer Sarum
Oxford Observed
Northumberland

TOWN
AND
TOWNSCAPE

Thomas Sharp

JOHN MURRAY

© THOMAS SHARP 1968

Printed in Great Britain for
John Murray, Albemarle Street, London
by Jarrold & Sons Ltd, Norwich
7195 1799 0

TO RACHEL

CONTENTS

ILLUSTRATIONS

PREFATORY NOTE

This is a book about the physical character of our English towns, about the way they look, about what is destroying their looks, and in part about a particular way of enjoying their looks. One cannot sensibly deal with visual things without using examples by way of illustration. My choice of examples may be open to criticism. It has been suggested to me that my frequent and detailed use of Oxford by way of example is too restrictive. But the town one knows best is generally the town where one lives: and if that town happens to be, as in my view Oxford is, one of the great towns of the world (even though I owe it no personal loyalties) it would seem to me to be better to use the best examples of what one knows best, especially when these may be the best examples there are, rather than use less good examples that one knows less well merely to attempt a universality where that is in any case impossible.

Part of the text relating to Oxford townscape is based on chapters in *Oxford Observed* (Country Life Ltd., 1952, now out of print). The section dealing with tower buildings is mainly from a report commissioned by the Cambridgeshire County Council and published as an article in *The Town Planning Review*, vol. XXXIII, no. 4, January 1963. Some of the illustrations have also appeared in those publications.

I thank my publisher for many valuable suggestions; and the following for free permission to use copyright illustrations (the numbers referring to pages):

Ministry of Housing & Local Government, 115; National Buildings Record, 20, 88, 89, 90; Exeter Corporation, 117; Oxford Corporation, 46 lower, 47, 48, 49, 51, 53, 54, 57, 58, 59, 60, 65, 103; Cambridgeshire & Isle of Ely County Council, 28, 29, 127;

INTRODUCTION

These are critical times for our towns; the most critical in all their long history. Never before have there been so many different influences for change operating so strongly upon them at the same time. And never before has the tempo of possible change been so swift and so pressing.

The influences for change are partly social needs, partly mere fashion. They operate over the whole extent of a town, but mainly upon its older parts, the town-centre, the commercial and public-social localities.

The ever-increasing motor traffic makes the magnetic attraction of the town-centre more widespread and at the same time diminishes the quality of its attractiveness. The car enables people individually to get there more readily, but collectively frustrates them when they arrive. The old streets cannot, without increasing discomfort, accommodate the cars that are driven into them – discomfort to the people in the cars and to the people trying to get about outside them. The cars, whether they are being driven or are standing, obstruct the views of the town as well as movement about it. To attempt to accommodate them, old streets are widened in bits and pieces, new roads are driven disruptively through old localities, gaping holes are made in street frontages and elsewhere to provide parking places. The physical character and appearance of the town is being changed – and always it seems for the worse. It is being changed by a new intensification of a recently grown influence (recent as town-time goes) in the absence of a considered whole policy of dealing with it.

Another social change is a change of emphasis and of practice in the activity in which a town-centre is mainly

Elm Hill, Norwich. A pleasantly curving diversified street; two foiling trees; textured road surface. But should it be used for parking cars?

I

engaged, the activity of trading. The multiple store, the
supermarket and similar new trading establishments require
different and bigger buildings than have hitherto been usual
in the streets of the older towns; and they have a marked
effect on the appearance of those streets. And at the same
time and in a wider sense they can exert influences which
are strangely contradictory. Besides those that establish
themselves in town-centres, where they not only change the
physical character of their setting but increase the traffic
converging on it, some of them now establish themselves
in suburban localities, or even in the countryside on the
edge of a town, seeking for their own purposes to avoid
rather than add to congestion. That kind of establishment

2

has not yet become common in Britain, although it is already widespread in America. If it does develop here, there will be the probability that while it may have the beneficial result of reducing to some extent the congestion in the town-centre to which it is satellite, it may also have the detrimental one of eroding from that centre the functions which have historically been associated with it, and so reduce it to a place that is neither wholly dead nor fully alive.

If the town is to survive in anything like the character in which we have known it, the influences that these and similar changes exert must be countered by measures and actions that will remove the conditions that bring them into being or adapt them to a more acceptable form than they now have. That need not be difficult if people can be brought to accept reasonable discipline in place of unreasonable licence. Certainly the acceptance of new disciplines in the ways of getting about a town is essential. And something of the same sort of acceptance will be necessary on the part of those responsible for the form of much of the physical change, the architects and owners of the new buildings which are having such disruptive effect in so many places.

Horsham, Sussex. The main shopping street of a country town become a battlefield.

It is through the architects and their clients that the influence of mere fashion has had, and is having, its effect – fashion in street buildings that either lack street perspective or are hopelessly at odds with established building-rhythms; in tower-buildings that are wholly out of scale and character with the towns over which they exert architectural tyranny. In these new buildings all previous acceptance of something like a collective discipline has been rejected. It has been rejected through an architectural arrogance in which the general character of the town or a street is considered of no importance compared with the intoxication of self-assertion and self-advertisement. If the changes brought about by traffic and new forms of trading are regrettable, they at least have a functional foundation in that they arise out of the satisfaction of social needs; and while creating problems and causing disruption in some respects they confer social benefits in others. But the damage and destruction caused by mere architectural fashion has no such defence. It is simply

3

Introduction

a betrayal by some architects – whether through ignorance or indifference – of both their social and their wider aesthetic responsibilities.

Added to these influences for change is the increase of tempo at which change now takes place. Hitherto rebuilding in most towns has been small in scale and slow in pace – a single new building in a street here and there, a new shop front or two over a long period. Even where large-scale changes seemed necessary there were not then the agencies available to make them. Now, suddenly, large-scale re-building has become a rewarding activity for financial speculators. There is money in it – a great deal of money. Financial corporations, insurance companies, property tycoons search round the country for town-centres to 'redevelop'. They compete in elaborately prepared designs and in inducements to persuade town councils to facilitate their activities through the use of legislative powers which they do not themselves possess, throwing in a new town-hall, a new swimming-bath, or a theatre, as a gift in return for services rendered. A small speculator with an eye for profitable sites and a persuasive way with banks, investment corporations and town councils, can become a millionaire in a few years through this kind of activity. There has been nothing like it since the building of the railways. Whether it is likely to continue to be good business or not is for financiers and economists to decide. Whether it is likely to be for the social good is a matter which only time will tell. But that it is having powerful effects on the character of many of our towns is obvious for all to see.

The effects are most striking in the older towns, for it is there that the changes in building forms are most obviously disruptive. Protests and pleas for preservation are sometimes heard. They are not heard anything like as often as would once have seemed probable. And even when they are made it is generally for the wrong reasons, for the preservation of the sentimentally picturesque rather than the visually important. That the changes are being accepted with less resistance than might be expected is largely because of people's sheer bewilderment – bewilderment at the speed with which things are done, and bewilderment as to what is

Alnwick, Northumberland: plan. The pattern of streets, curving, straightening, narrowing, widening: and a small market square, M.

4

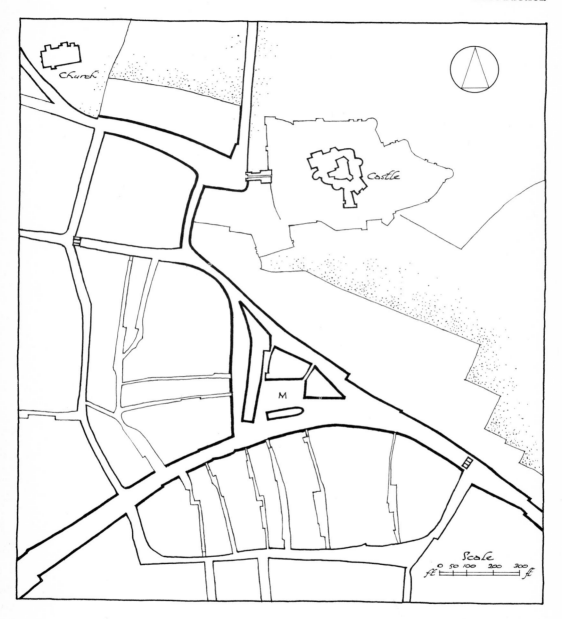

right or wrong, what is good or bad, in modern building. The principles of good town-building, an understanding of the nature of town character, an informed appreciation of

Introduction

even the mere looks of a town have perhaps never been very highly developed among the general run of citizens – certainly they have not been so for the last hundred years and more. And now that many architects themselves seem to have abandoned interest in them, these critical times for our towns, particularly our older towns, are likely, unless there is a rapid change of attitude, to mean the end of something in which we in England once showed a natural genius – the genius of creating towns that nearly always have had a whole character; that generally have had pleasantness and seemliness; that often, even, have had a quite remarkable beauty; that always have maintained a comfortable human scale (even if not a comfortable size); that like us, their creators, have remained disciplined in freedom, orderly even in variety. It will mean the end of all that; and the completion of the urban chaos, the physical disorder, the architectural anarchy that is already far advanced in the larger cities.

In the pages which follow, an attempt is made to analyse how the physical character of a town[1] is constituted; and how that character, how the *looks* of a town, may best be observed and appreciated. That analysis will not be concerned with town-planning in its wider aspects, nor with architecture as such. It will deal simply with the physical character of towns; with the urban scenery of good English towns in general and some exemplary ones in particular; with the way towns look, and with some of the conditions which affect their looks and the possibilities of enjoying those looks. In regarding towns in this way it will not be a matter of dealing merely with superficialities or extrinsic values. How a town looks is no less important than how it works; and if in making a town work we destroy its looks we destroy a large part of its intrinsic value to our civilization.

---

[1] Throughout it is the closely built part of a town, the town-centre, that is referred to. Suburban areas present different problems. It would be cumbersome to keep referring to 'town-centres' merely to distinguish them from suburbs; so 'town' used here means the close-knit central part of a town.

FACE AND FIGURE

I UNITY IN VARIETY

Walking in the central parts of the medium-sized or smaller towns of England, especially in the midlands or the south, one makes a very varied progress through differing urban scenes. The High Street, where the main shops are, will probably be a longish street. It will almost certainly be somewhat irregular in its configuration. Here and there, there will be a jut or recession in the building-lines. Somewhere along its course there will be a swelling or a narrowing of the roadway. The two sides of the street will not often be exactly parallel; and in their alignments, though not in the kinds of building that front them, they may even seem to have a curious independence of each other. Sometimes there may be a break among the buildings for the forecourt of the Council Offices, or a chapel or something of that kind: and a tree may lean out there with a happy softening effect on the scene. Somewhere along the street, or perhaps at its ends, there will be a curve or a turning away from the straight, so that the view is contained within the street itself, even though the main feature in it, the spire of the parish church, is seen some distance beyond, rising over a tumble of intermediate roofs.

At its end where the Guildhall stands, the High Street may divide into two short narrow streets whose ends are quite hidden. Probably there will be an overlarge-looking signpost saying to what distant towns they are leading: but as someone walking in this particular town for his own local purposes, and not interested in the least in the way to Westchester or Eastbury or even London, the observer may well wish they need not be there at all. Taking his chosen one of these two streets, he may come to a market-

Ledbury, Herefordshire. A gunnel leading from High Street to parish church.

9

Face and figure

place, with an old cross or a small open-sided market-building not quite in the middle. After the shut-in-ness of the High Street and the narrow street he has just come by, he may now experience a pleasant sense of change, even of release, at seeing a new opening of space and a widened expanse of sky – and he may still experience it, if only in a half-conscious way, even if as a native or a long resident of the town he has seen it hundreds of times before. And he will experience it yet again, with an added difference, when he has taken the high-walled gunnel which is the short-cut from there, and has come into the squarer-shaped and more regular open *place*[1] in front of the parish church – the added difference being not only in the different shape

Chichester, Sussex. A richly complex urban scene. Cathedral, trees, market cross, main shopping streets. (Country Life)

[1] It is a deficiency of our English terms that we have no general word to mean a particular kind of space surrounded by buildings in the sense of the French *place* or the Italian *piazza*. 'Square' suggests too regular a shape for forms which may be entirely irregular. 'Place' in our sense (except as 'market-place') may mean anything from a particular spot to a whole town, or even nowadays, mistakenly, an entire country. So town-planners are driven to give the word a French pronunciation in speech and italics in print.

Diss, Norfolk. Market-place, with church on rising ground.

of the *place* but in the form it takes – the grassed space in the middle, the fine trees round the sides, and the similar though not quite equal Georgian terraced houses that line them; houses which in their calm composure provide a complement by contrast to the varied streets and the varied market-place behind.

The variousness experienced in this short walk, besides lying in the differences in the widths alignments and configurations of the streets themselves, in the difference between them and the open *places*, and even in the difference between the general run of streets and the occasional composed group of more ordered frontages – the variousness in an English town of this kind lies also, and perhaps even more strikingly, in the architecture of the buildings lining the streets.

These buildings will almost all be in small-unit frontages. And they will have a most telling variety of form and treatment. There will be old red brickwork with painted reveals to the window openings and white-painted window-framing. There will be variously colour-washed plaster, painted brick, half-timber-and-plaster. According to the district there may be stone, flint, clap-boarding, hung-tiles, hung-slates. Such public buildings as occur will generally be stone-built. Standing ranged together, these various treatments of wall surfaces give the streets a richly diversified effect. And as there are variations in material, there are also moderate variations in building heights. Eaves lines or ridge lines rarely run equally for more than two or three frontages. Gables and dormers further break up already broken roof-lines. The irregularity of building-lines add to the varied effect. Irregularity of form and frontage combines with changes of material to produce complexity and variety.

The small-unit frontages have, of course, risen out of function. The buildings are mostly comparatively small shops – shops of widely varying kinds: specializing shops, family affairs, local businesses. Occasionally an hotel or a small emporium's façade, a post-office or a bank, may introduce a rather longer frontage. But generally even these are not so pronounced as to disturb in any violent way the general rhythm of the frontages, the general rhythm of the street. That *rhythm* is the essential constituent in the character of streets like these. In spite of their variousness in materials, in broken roof-lines, in irregular building-lines and so on, each street has something of a common rhythm that constitutes it as a whole in a single even though complex character. And there is another characteristic that has helped in this – the common form of the fenestration in the upper floors above the shop-fronts; the interplay of solid wall and square or vertically rectangular void which has hitherto been the general way of building. Though windows may be at varying levels, their similarity of form within their probably differently-surfaced surrounding walls has been a further constituent in keeping a common character, in maintaining the similar general rhythm.

Thus there are two forms of variousness that do much to constitute the character of these older towns. There is the variety of plan-form; the variety that exists between broad

Henley, Oxon. A wide main street, a one-time market-place, curving gently as it reaches the parish church. Buildings of various periods and various materials: the rhythm largely maintained by similar window openings.

streets, narrow streets, different kinds of irregularly aligned streets, between open *places* compared with these, and in the differences between open *places* themselves. That is the variety of contrast. And there is besides that, and more common than it, the variety in the buildings within the streets and *places* themselves, variety that is not so much of contrast but *variety within the same kind*, *variety within an established rhythm*, variety (one might almost say) within similarity, within a broad unity of character.

It is that that is the quintessence of the physical character of the generality of the older towns of England. Their character is established in variousness. It is variety that has given them their liveliness, their charm, their frequent gaiety, their easy grace, their comfortable friendly quality. Yet it is a variousness that has its natural restraints, its reserves, its reticences. It is a variousness that makes an acknowledgement of form, that still has within itself a recognition and acceptance of the virtues of orderliness. It

13

is not a variety between extremes: not the wild undisciplined variety that makes the centres of most American smaller cities and towns, for example, such a nightmare of disorder. It is a variety that reflects the long-developing well-settled self-disciplined society of its creators, as well as changing architectural history. It is variety within a basic unity – a unity which is established and maintained through an overall rhythm operating within a broadly common character of form.

That, in a general way, is something of the general character of our older towns, the medium-sized towns, the cathedral-cities, the market-towns, the country towns of England. It is perhaps rash to make even this generalization. It would be rasher still to generalize about our towns as a whole. Even leaving aside the nineteenth-century industrial towns as something special and far outside our consideration here, there are too many kinds of town to permit of any worthwhile generalization about them all – variations in kind and size from the great metropolis of millions, through the cities of a mere million or so, down to the little country town of a couple of thousand inhabitants. The larger cities and towns are at once so complex and so amorphous as almost to defy any attempt at a generalized analysis of what constitutes their character – if indeed they have much individual character today. And even in this one type of town that we have been glancing at, the generalized picture does not always hold – does not even always hold for the part of England, the more southern part, where it is more common. There are as many variations of even that kind of town as there are different towns. Every town differs from every other town; every High Street from every other High Street. But all the same we may justly adopt Pope's lines[1] to describe these towns in general as places

> Where order in variety we see,
> And where, tho' all things differ, all agree.

Stamford, Lincs. An old street with buildings of various heights, but the rhythm maintained.

But besides this general type of varied town there does exist another type, uncommon though it may be – the town or quarter of a town which is its direct opposite in that it is

[1] From *Windsor Forest*, describing landscape.

14

constituted in the deliberately composed unity of identical elements rather than in variety. The formal street, crescent and square do not often occur in our High Streets; but they are not entirely uncommon in localities near by. And in

certain whole quarters of a few towns they are so frequent
and in such continuity as to constitute the essential character
of the environment. Bath, and the whole consistent quarter
of Edinburgh that is still called The New Town two hundred years after its building began, are prime examples of
this kind of town-building in Britain. But a multitude of
streets and squares in London, a considerable part of the
central area of Newcastle upon Tyne (perhaps the most
extensive single quarter built from the first for commercial
purposes), and numbers of Georgian and Regency streets
and squares scattered here and there in many towns
throughout the country, are in striking contrast to the other,
the general, kind of town-building.

The difference between these formal compositions and
the more 'natural' varied streets lies not only in the regularity
of their buildings. It lies also in the regularity of the plan-
forms to which they subscribe. It is the two together which

produce the particular effects where, to adopt other lines from Pope,

> No single parts unequally surprise,
> All comes united to th' admiring eyes.[1]

These effects are fixed and finite. All buildings in them sub-scribe as individual units to a single predetermined over-riding design. Not only are they regular in their design pattern; their materials are the same throughout each particular composition, throughout the street, the square, the circus, the crescent – even throughout the whole quarter. The parts must hold together as a whole. Any striking change in one of the parts, a change of design-pattern, of material, of height in any one of the units, will destroy the total effect. The effect here must be total or it does not exist. Variety is only possible between individual squares crescents and whole streets (and even then chiefly in plan-form and design, and only very moderately in material or height) – is only possible *between* the unities, not within them.

Brighton. Formal unity. A terrace, which would be disrupted by any new building not of the same form and material.

So, then, we have these two types of town, or of town-quarters: the informal varied type to which all but a small fraction of our towns belong – the type where unity of character still exists within variety of form: that, and the other comparatively infrequent type, the formally composed kind, where unity exists in closely ordered identity of design. In both these kinds of town there is more often than not seemliness and pleasantness. There is sometimes even beauty. There is almost always a settled character. All these qualities are now being threatened by change. Through indifference or inadequacy we can let that change destroy them in the character we have known. Or if we value that character we can keep it in being. We can keep it in being sometimes by the actual preservation of buildings that play an important part in it, but more generally by seeing that new buildings subscribe to the disciplines within which it is constituted. It is a choice of one or the other. And it is ours to decide which it shall be.

[1] From *Essay on Criticism,* though here Pope was speaking of a single architectural feature, the dome.

II MAINTENANCE OF CHARACTER

Towns are living organisms. Their buildings must serve contemporary needs. In so far as they seriously fail to meet those needs they must be modified and adapted to do so; and if they are incapable of reasonable modification and adaptation to modern use they must be replaced.

That at least is sound reason from a utilitarian point of view. And buildings must certainly have a basis in utility. But they cannot, in a civilized society, be judged wholly according to whether or not they are in a state of perfect usefulness. They are also objects: objects of character, personality, and a physical appearance which, according to the kind of society they serve, may be as important, with a different kind of importance, as their mere usefulness may be. Their associations, as well as their appearance, may also be regarded as important – important as part of the history of the society that built them and has used them.

In considering what should happen to the older streets and the older individual buildings in our towns, the matter that has to be decided, therefore, is the degree of value we attach to them as they are now. We have a multitude of streets of a certain settled and attractive character, great numbers of buildings about them of architectural distinction, a host of buildings of historical association and importance – streets and buildings that are still reasonably capable of serving modern needs or of being adapted to serve them. These possessions we have now – they are here with us, existing, realized, in actual physical presence. Shall we let them go? Shall we exchange the certain good of the present, where it exists, for an uncertain distant future and a long period of intermediate anarchy? In the end it is as straight-forward and direct a question as that.

There are several possible attitudes of mind that can be adopted. At one extreme it can be argued that these streets and these quarters should be totally rebuilt to meet modern needs – and since today's needs are unlikely to be the same as those a few decades hence, they should even be rebuilt in a manner that would make them expendable in a generation or two. Clearly such wholesale rebuilding over a short period is impossible in any event – impossible financially, impossible physically because of the labour involved, impossible socially because of the chaotic disturbance that would be created. The total rebuilding of our grim indus-trial towns would indeed be very welcome, if it were pos-sible. But even if it were a possibility, the rebuilding of the towns that we are concerned with here would be totally unacceptable by anyone who has any care for the visual qualities, the architectural and social history and the sheer physical pleasantness that they nearly always display.

Then there is the possible attitude of letting things go hang, of letting redevelopment rip in places and localities where it is profitable, of letting present needs and present architectural modes express themselves regardless of what individual buildings may be lost or what the effect on the character of their surviving surroundings may be. This is the attitude which is producing the damage that is becoming common today, the damage that will indeed end in visual anarchy and historical emptiness if it is continued much longer – the attitude which, at Gosport, for example, has resulted, in less than twenty years, in the demolition of more than 100 of the 130 buildings officially listed as of archi-tectural and historical interest and importance, and in the establishment, in their place, of a modern neutrality where once there was grace and individual character.

In diametric opposition to that, there is the attitude which deplores and opposes change of almost any kind, which is based more on a sentimental conservatism than on visual evaluation. This is the opposite attitude of extremism – the attitude that produces impatience among those who are all for modernization at any cost and that at the same time

19

Gosport, Hants.
Chapel Row: 1953.

does much to discredit those who take a more temperate and practical view of what should and can be done. This extreme preservationist attitude is in the end self-defeating, for it fails to face up not only to what is practical but to what is actually necessary and desirable in the living organism that every town must be.

Against these extreme attitudes there is the one which, acknowledging the desirability of maintaining character, seeks actual preservation only where that is in a high degree important, and for the rest admits the inevitability of some new building and redevelopment taking place and asks only that, when it is undertaken where there is existing unity of character, it should accept the disciplines that have brought that unity about. Though this attitude does in part seek actual preservation of the more important existing structures, it is *maintenance of character* that is generally aimed at. As such it is different from the more rigid preservationist attitude. The difference needs to be emphasized; and it can be clarified by describing the intention as conservation rather than preservation.

In the general policy of conservation the actual physical preservation that may be desirable relates to both the formal compositions in street square and crescent that have been referred to, and to certain other groups and individual buildings. Clearly where unity exists through the repetition of identical elements, as in the formal groupings, the character of the total composition can only be maintained by maintaining the form as a whole. To maintain the form

Gosport.
Chapel Row: 1966.

as a whole, the form of each unit and each part of each unit must be maintained.

In these formal compositions preservation may require comprehensive measures. The total unity that is their characteristic was generally only achieved through comprehensive activity by one builder or agency. Where, as is generally the case, the individual units of the composition have now passed to a multiplicity of owners of whom some are unwilling or unable to accept the disciplines required to keep the unity in being, it may be necessary not merely to exercise control through the operation of town-planning powers, but for the ownership of the whole or of parts to be publicly acquired in the public interest. And of course what is important, in all these cases where preservation is necessary for reasons of town character, is the façades that are presented to public view. The preservation of the interiors of buildings is a different matter; and one that we are not concerned with here.

It may have to be like that, too, where actual preservation, not merely conservation, is necessary to maintain character in another sense. There are ranges of buildings in many old towns that contribute so much to the character of the town as a whole that that character would suffer serious damage or loss if they were destroyed. Or there are buildings which, even though they may not themselves be of outstanding architectural or historical interest, are important to the setting of some particular scene or some special building or group of buildings. Here it may sometimes be not so much

their own inherent value that requires their preservation as fear of what, in present circumstances, may take their place – the need to let well alone. In these kinds of buildings, too, as in the formal kind, it may be necessary to undertake internal adaptation and rehabilitation to make them satisfactory for modern use. Again it is the public face of the building that is important in town character. And here again the only way to keep that may be by the public paying for its preservation.

But while actual preservation may be necessary and desirable in special cases like these, it cannot be undertaken to maintain the character of the good ordinary streets in good ordinary towns. Nor should it be. In seeking the maintenance of character in these good ordinary streets, and in condemning certain modern building forms where they have gone wrong, there need be no suggestion that modern architecture as such is inevitably disruptive there, and that new buildings should be designed in imitation of the old.

Bewdley, Worcs. Unity through rhythm of frontages. The scene contained by the siting of the church, the road swinging round it. (Country Life)

22

Farnham, Surrey. Unity of dissimilar elements through common building materials and fenestration forms. (Country Life)

It would be absurd and stultifying to suggest anything of that kind. It is their hospitality to change that has made our High Streets what they are, that has established the variousness that is their essential character. New buildings must be accepted where they are essential in such streets. There is no reason why, well designed within the existing disciplines, they should not add to their character and enhance their pleasantness. But if they are to do that, if indeed they are to be acceptable at all, they must acknowledge those disciplines. And the main discipline that has to be accepted is the maintenance of the rhythm of the street.

There is, however, an additional discipline that may have to be acknowledged. We have been speaking of town-building as being of two main types – the type where unity of character lies in identity of form, and that where unity exists in variety. There is also an intermediate type which shares some of the characteristics of both. The Cotswold towns are examples that immediately spring to mind.

Face and figure

Chipping Campden, Broadway, Stow-on-the-Wold, Chipping Norton, Moreton-in-Marsh achieve their total effects as much because they are built throughout of similar materials in wall and roof as because of the quality of their by no means unvaried architectural design. Some northern hill-towns, though generally less distinguished in their architecture and of a sterner character, are the same. Here, though the preservation of actual form may not be as necessary as in the formal compositions, maintenance of character in rebuilding may require the use of materials identical or very similar to those used for the present buildings.

But as has been said, the main discipline that has to be accepted against disruption of character in the town where unity still exists in variety is the maintenance of the rhythm of the street – the main discipline, that is, as regards the

Broadway, Worcs. Unity through common materials and forms.

*Warkworth, North-
umberland. The castle
dominates, but the cars
intrude.*

hitherto normal method of building in street formation, for
there are other causes of disruption affecting far more than
the individual street, affecting indeed wide areas of a town
or even a town as a whole – causes which we must later
consider separately and in detail.

The disruptions that are breaking the rhythm of so many
streets in our older towns operate in two ways. They break
the rhythm of short-unit frontages by introducing long-
frontage buildings among them. They also break it, even in
short-unit frontages, by changes in detailed design to forms
which are at odds with existing forms. As a result of their
form and design they have introduced, not the acceptable
variations within which a broad unity may still exist, but
unacceptable discontinuities and disunities which destroy
the established rhythms.

Take the changes in detailed design first. The main
change of design which affects rhythm is in the form of
window openings. Hitherto the common form of these has
been square or vertically rectangular. That is their form
in almost all buildings older than a decade or two. The

25

Face and figure

repetition of this form of window down a street, even though the openings be at somewhat varying levels, is one of the strongest elements in establishing the street's rhythm. Equally, of course, a strong rhythm could be established by other forms used in continuity – by horizontally emphasized rather than vertically emphasized openings. It would be a different kind of rhythm: but it might be an acceptable one in its own right: it might be acceptable in a new street (especially in a new town). But the horizontal form is so strongly in opposition to the vertical form that its unconsidered introduction into an established rhythm of vertical forms is bound to introduce disruption into that rhythm. And that is exactly what is happening in many places through the obsession of some architects with their own individual designs regardless of the situation to which they are being applied.

Another cause of disruption even in the small-unit frontage derives from an even more elementary error in architectural design – the error which is concerned only with direct elevational effect in mind, forgetful of the effect of perspective. This occurs in the kind of building where the main part of the façade is set so deeply behind the structural elements (which become encased like fins) that the recessed parts disappear altogether in a side-long view. What happens then is that the building appears merely as a lump of dead wallage in the street-picture – a most solid and disruptive interruption to its rhythm.

But if these and similar disruptions caused by the unsatisfactory rebuilding of a single small-unit frontage or a run of two or three such frontages are regrettable, disruption on a far greater scale is caused when the rebuilding of a whole block of small frontages creates a few large-unit frontages in its place. This, as has been said, is mainly brought about through the new type of building required for chain-stores, supermarkets, departmental-stores, office-blocks with ground-floor shops, and so on.

Since an example may be more illuminating than generalities, a rebuilding of this kind which has taken place in recent years at Cambridge may be cited. And, in regarding it as an example, it should be borne in mind that it has been

Oxford. Disruption by destruction of rhythm in frontage length and window openings.

Oxford. Disruption through introduction of over-long frontages and the ignoring of effects in perspective.

Cambridge. Street scene c. 1956. The change begun in the demolition of the corner building.

even more disastrous there than if it had occurred in a more normal town – more disastrous because the existence of variety in the town streets of such a place is more than usually necessary in order to provide, through contrast to the long-frontaged near-formal college and university buildings, the architectural foils which are an essential ingredient of university-town character.

What has happened at Cambridge is that a whole collection of buildings situated between two colleges has been demolished to make room for two single new buildings occupying the site. Until seven or eight years ago there was a hundred-yard-long building block composed of an extraordinarily varied range of mostly eighteenth- and early nineteenth-century domestic buildings. These were of comparatively short individual frontages with a much broken building-line, and were unusually varied in height. While some of the buildings were of considerable architectural interest in the narrower sense, the general collection as a whole could not claim to be. It was a bit of a jumble.

28

Cambridge. The scene from the same point, a year or two later. The change completed.

Nevertheless, it made a valuable contribution to the university-town architectural scene. It did so particularly as a foil to the neighbouring college buildings. Its return frontage, to a small street at right angles to the main street, was different again – very different. It comprised a fifty-yard-long run of eight cottage-type houses, two-storeys high with dormers in a tiled mansard roof. Their façades were plastered and colour-washed. In their continuity of similar windows in both wall and roof they presented a modest uniformity that was in marked and foiling contrast both to the scale and formality of the college across the narrow street and to the scale and jumbled street-and-roof lines of the main-street buildings round the corner. Here was a valuable remaining instance of an essential interplay between the main constituents of the university-town scene: an interplay that is now by no means as common as it used to be and should be.

One would have thought that this was just the kind of scene that was so valuable to the boasted university-town

29

character of Cambridge that everything possible would have
been done to maintain it in being. But no: the whole considerable complex, and its contribution to the town, has
been swept away. In its place, in place of all this small-unit
varied foil to larger buildings, there have been erected two
large-unit buildings: one of overbearing bulk and monstrous
pomposity; the other, incongruously lower, crouching like
a shivering orphan nephew beside it, but still, in its un-
broken large-unit frontage, too like the college next door
to contribute anything but dullness to the scene. And as
sad as the result is the way it has come about. For this was
no crime committed by blind and uncontrolled commercial
interests that had no responsibility to the town. It was
undertaken by one of the colleges of the University (though
not for college purposes – except financial ones). And it was
approved by the Royal Fine Art Commission which was
established precisely to prevent such architectural disasters.

Not unlike this rebuilding, though often on a larger scale,
is the 'comprehensive redevelopment' that is taking place in
other towns in various parts of the country and that is planned
for many more. And it is this – this 'comprehensive redevelopment' as it is at present practised and envisaged –
that is the greatest of the disruptions that threaten the
character of these older towns we are considering. It may be
very welcome elsewhere – in the industrial towns for example.
In the other towns with the settled character of unity in
variety it can be disruptive in the extreme.

Frequently it is being undertaken for no other reason than
the profit of property speculators: not for public good arising
out of public need. Sometimes it may indeed be necessary
because wholesale dilapidation has gone too far to be
recovered, because adaptation to modern needs is too difficult
to undertake, or because modern needs such as those of
transport require it – though proposals based on these and
similar arguments should not be too readily accepted for they
are frequently unjustified. But where the demand for wholesale rebuilding is indeed irresistible it needs to be of a
different kind from the brutal and unimaginative comprehensive redevelopment which today has no regard for the
character of the town in which it is situated. A new concept

*Winchester. New
buildings integrated in
their setting with the old.*

30

*Winchester. New and old
sitting nicely together.*

is required here. The idea of 'comprehensive redevelopment' is always advanced as the architects' and town-planners' inspired correction of the sins of 'piecemeal redevelopment'. But if 'piecemeal redevelopment' has become a dirty phrase in the planners' dictionary, it was nevertheless precisely that kind of activity that produced the kinds of streets we have in these towns today – the best as well as the worst. So something of a conjunction of the two concepts is required. What is to be avoided is the one single comprehensive design applied on too large a scale and for too great a length. What should be sought for is the individual rebuilding of the various units of short frontage within the required comprehensive plan. It will be far less easy to do this than simply to design and build one large building or complex of large

33

Salisbury. Similarity of height and window treatment secure integration of the new with the old.

buildings. And it will have its own dangers to be avoided – particularly the danger of falling into affectation or romanticism. But if the settled character of our older streets is to be maintained where large-scale rebuilding has to take place it can probably only be done in some such way as this.

Even so, there can be no denying the kinds of building that the development of new forms of trading requires – the supermarkets and such like. The way to accommodate those while maintaining the character of the old streets is surely to provide adjoining places where they will form complexes of their own, with their own common character. Such an arrangement would, indeed, not only avoid the disruption that now occurs, but could actually enrich the town by way of a contrast of form – a different, broader-based, variation than the detailed variousness which the present streets provide. Such contrasts of form sometimes occurred in the past – occurred where, say, a formal Georgian square or crescent was built just off an old informal High Street. There was a splendid example of it at Exeter, before the blitz of 1942, where the urbane and flowing unity of the late eighteenth-century Bedford Circus most strikingly and successfully adjoined the medieval High Street. Other examples still exist today. And if these examples from the past were mainly domestic rather than commercial quarters, that does not in any way lessen their relevance as an indication of what could now be done with equally successful effect for a different purpose.

These are some of the considerations that might help to save the character of our old towns in the plans that are being made for them and in the rebuilding that is taking place. But as well as the positive disruptions that we have been looking at, there is another more insidious danger to that character. It lies in slow deterioration through unrelated actions over a period of time.

An example of that can be taken from what has occurred at Chippenham in Wiltshire. There an unusual range of several monumental country-town buildings of great character standing in a main street has been broken down and supplanted over a period of years by modern shops. It

Chippenham, Wilts. Robust and fine-scaled buildings in the High Street, 1929.

The first building comes down, and the rot begins. The same scene, five years later.

The rot extends relentlessly: 1955: and instead of the old fine robustness we have a cheap and vulgar insipidity.

34

is, of course, as has been said, a different kind of disruption from the kind we have been looking at: and it leads to a different kind of consideration. If the new buildings had been good of their kind, objection might have been limited

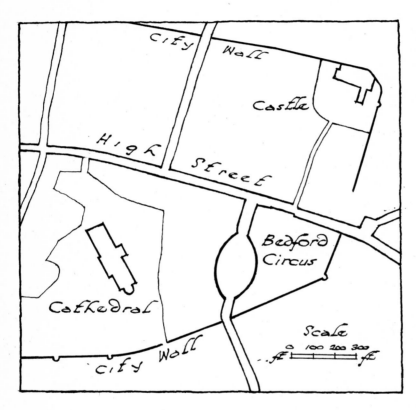

Exeter: plan: Bedford Circus (destroyed by bombing; 1942): a formal composition adjoining the old informal High Street.

to regret at the loss of fine buildings of historical interest, rather than to the change of character which the removal has involved. As it is, what one mainly feels is shame and despair that what has replaced buildings of such quality should be as mean and ignoble as the new ones are – and this in an age when the architectural design of new buildings is supposed to be subject to control in the public interest.

For in the end the fate of our towns lies largely in the hands of our architects.

TOWN AND TOWNSCAPE

III   A WAY OF LOOKING

So far we have looked only at the disruption that occurs through unacceptable building forms imposed upon streets of settled character. We need also to look at the two more dramatic kinds of disruption that have been indicated – forms of disruption that are threatening every kind and size of town; disruption by motors and high buildings. But before we do that it may be useful to look at a few selected towns by way of example to see how particular existing effects are created within general character. And as well as looking at them it may be helpful to consider also what is the best way of looking so as to see and appreciate them best.

The best way of looking to see them best. What does that imply? The way to see a town, it may be said, is the ordinary one of simply looking at it as one goes about it, noticing such buildings as may perhaps be particularly striking, particularly good (or bad), and getting a general impression of it as a whole. That is certainly one way – and the general way. But it is a limited way. There is another, by which one may see much more. That way is by looking not merely at the scenes but at the scenery.

It is an odd thing that there has not hitherto been a term to describe the changing collective views one gets in going about a town. There has been no word to describe urban scenery. Country scenery has long had its definitive term – and a very evocative one at that – in *landscape*. The scenery of the sea is sometimes called seascape. Even sky-scenery has been thought to need a special term. Only our terms for the scenery of the town have hitherto been clumsy and evasive.

While we commonly speak of the scenery, the landscape, of Barsetshire, we speak only of views in the city of Barset

Oxford. Holywell Street begins its long townscape-enriching curve: and two trees lean out as foils to the buildings.

39

itself. But as a single country scene, a country-view, is merely part of the larger panorama which we call landscape, so is a street-scene but a part of whatever we may like to call the urban counterpart of landscape. In the absence of any established term adequately to describe that, it is only recently that a new one, the adaptation of the term 'landscape' to 'townscape'[1] has begun to supply it.

It would be surprising that we have managed for so long without this term identifying landscape's urban counterpart, were it not that the very concept of it seems hardly to have existed in any conscious sense.

The reason no doubt is partly that it is more or less impossible to see or apprehend extensive parts of a town at any one time, in the way one can generally see extensive parts of a landscape. But partly it is also that only monumental urban scenes, or very romantic ones, have been thought worthy of special appreciation. In the main those are the scenes that have been consciously created under the formal kind of town-building which we have already referred to – either those or scenes whose impact arises from elements other than mere buildings and their arrangement. Almost invariably the effect of these scenes has been in the main static. The more formal building arrangements have been deliberately designed and created to produce set spectacular effects. Even the 'romantic' urban scenes which are especially admired tend to have a static character (or to be generally apprehended in that way). That spectacular street in Edinburgh, Princes Street, which is in such contrast to the New Town behind, is of this kind – though it hardly exists as a true *street* architecturally, but is essentially a *prospect*. It is these kinds of scenes, special, spectacular and unusual as they are, that have in the main been regarded as the only ones worthy of particular note and appreciation in a town. And this special regard for them must have contributed consider-

Morpeth, Northumberland. Delineation in drawing and engraving, and photography by the 'still' camera, must have helped to establish the apprehension of a town as a series of static views.

[1] The word 'townscape' has come into use of recent years among town-planners and architects. But it has generally been used either to denote a single street-scene or the collection of elements that constitute it – elements varying in size from large objects like buildings down to small ones of every kind, lamp-standards, telephone-boxes, bollards, fences, different kinds of paving. This imprecise use of the term is confusing. It would be better to stick to the term *street-scene* for the single scene, keeping *townscape* to mean the wider collective interconnecting ones that constitute town scenery. It is in this latter sense that the term is used here.

ably to the general experience and acceptance of town-scenery as something more or less static.

Another contributory cause may have been the manner in which town-scenery (as indeed country-scenery too) has necessarily been delineated by painters and draughtsmen. Unavoidably they have presented flat two-dimensional pictures of fixed and finite scenes. That is the very nature of drawing and painting. And in modern times the common camera has done the same. So, when eyes have been conditioned by paintings, drawings, photographs in books and picture-postcards, they have tended to see multifarious actuality as it has been presented in a single static representation. And if this has been more the case with town-scenery than with country-scenery that is no doubt because, again, of

the difficulty of visually experiencing an extensive part of a town at any one time.

Whatever the cause or causes, it is the case that the vast majority of us tend to see a town in this way – as a series of static scenes, a series of picture-postcard views. While we may appreciate the general collective character of a place, we tend to look at its buildings and other elements individually or in fixed compositions; to regard them as individual set scenes. We tend to look at them as single static three-dimensional pictures; three-dimensional still-lifes (to borrow a term from painting). We tend to use our eyes, in looking at them, like the lens of a still camera.

But there is another kind of camera which sees an altogether more comprehensive range of effects, which sees scenes very differently: sees them not as sharply separated individual pictures, but as a slow sequence of pictures melting and moving into and out of one another. This is the cinematograph or moving camera. And if we could come to use our eyes consciously in the town in the way we unconsciously do in the country, to use them more in the way of the moving than the still camera (realizing something of Oscar Wilde's paradox about nature imitating art, though in this case the attribute imitated would be a machine) – if we could adopt this different and unfamiliar though entirely natural and unconditioned way of looking, we would enormously increase the range of our visual experience of towns. What it amounts to, in short, is that apart from seeing individual buildings and the individual set scenes of a town, there is another kind of visual experience, and a very enriching one, to be gained by looking at the town in this quite different way: by seeing it, or at least extensive parts of it, in movement, as it were, as one moves about it. By seeing it not with the static but with the kinetic eye.

Perhaps what this means may best be realized by again referring to landscape. It will probably be agreed that the full pleasure of the countryside does not lie in a series of fixed and finite views. It is gained as one moves about. In walking, bicycling, travelling by train or car, one gets a far fuller range of landscape experience than in standing still in the middle of it. One sees a flowing succession of continuously changing pictures, with trees, hedges, fields, farmhouses, barns, byres, church towers, near and distant hills, clouds and a host of other features – one sees these in new positions and new relations to each other. This sense of movement and change is the true essence of landscape experience. And so it is to the urban counterpart of landscape.

The sense of movement is in the townscape itself. The fact that the movement belongs to the observer, rather than to the objects observed, is incidental and largely irrelevant. The important thing is that, as the observer moves, the buildings and other objects in view alter not only in the relation of their own parts but in their relations to the rest of their visible environment. Thus the limiting conception of the individual building or street-scene as a three-dimensional urban still-life is enormously extended. The townscape becomes anything but static, anything but a series of set scenes, a succession of architectural still-lifes. It becomes a living moving unfolding kinetic experience, becomes a complicated resolution of changing relations. Even on a straight street one sees immediate and distant buildings, church spires and towers, groups of trees, perhaps distant hills outside the town; and as one moves about, these are seen in new positions and in changing relations to each other. In a curved or irregular street one gets signally more extended and greatly enriched effects. In movement down such a street there is a continual unfolding. New buildings, new objects, new scenes come in and then sink back as the street curves. Street frontages, towers, spires, higher buildings, a tree leaning from a forecourt, a small open area, a narrow entry lane, perhaps even some distant feature in another part of the town, or in the country outside – these features deploy out from the sides of the street into the middle of the changing picture, stand revealed, perhaps even dominant, for a moment, resolve as it were about the picture, then sink back, recede, and are replaced by other features. In such streets, and indeed in any street, this way of looking can gain one a range of visual experience far wider and richer than is possible through the limiting familiar static point of view.

And an important point about it is this – the experience is not merely made richer in a town which possesses riches already. Perhaps the greatest gain in this way of looking is the enlargement it affords of one's visual appreciation in almost any town. In the near still-view of a street or other urban scene, the quality of detailed design in the elements of the composition, and the capacity to apprehend that quality (that is to say, generally, the understanding and appreciation of architecture in itself), are of central importance. In the kinetic view, in the townscape rather than the town-scene, they are less important. If the quality of design is good it will give added pleasure. If it is downright bad, to the discerning eye it will be so disturbing as to reduce or destroy one's pleasure while it remains in view. But in very few cases is architectural quality the main determining attribute in town-scape appreciation. It is the interest of the relations of the parts of the unfolding scenes, and of the change of relations, that matters. So the appreciation and enjoyment of townscape as such is not in the least limited to places where good archi-tecture exists, nor to those who have expert eyes to see it. It is a pleasure to be got in any town that has some interest of form; and it can be enjoyed by anyone who cares to enjoy it. It can be got in towns which have no single building of pronounced architectural merit. Hundreds of country towns as well as most larger cities will give it in a vivid degree. So even in some less or greater degree may most industrial towns. Townscape in this sense has interests, pleasures, even excitements, to offer in the most unpromising places. And this way of looking at it, this use of the kinetic eye, will per-ceive and receive them – will perceive and receive, sometimes, effects of a most exciting and revealing kind, but even at a more commonplace level will perceive interest and enliven-ment in scenes which otherwise, looked at half-blindly (because statically), may seem dull and unworthy of notice.

IV OXFORD OBSERVED

The best way of demonstrating a thesis may be by way of particular examples. And since the thesis advanced here is concerned with visual matters, it should, if possible be demonstrated in visual terms.

But a book is, of course, at a clear disadvantage for this purpose. It is the *kinetic* quality of townscape that we are concerned with, as against the more common experience of seeing the town as a series of set 'still' views. And a book's pictures can only be still pictures. So one has to try to suggest the movement which is characteristic of good townscape by its very opposite. Nevertheless, even still photographs are better than nothing for aiding a verbal description of sights –so long as they are merely regarded as *aids*. And if we take as examples a few townscapes which illustrate to a special degree the distinctive qualities and characteristics that are to be demonstrated, that also should help to overcome the difficulty to some extent.

As a beginning we can take Oxford, the finest example of interrelated townscape in Britain, and one of the finest anywhere in the world. And in beginning with Oxford we can begin with the very essence of the thing in a concentrated example of tremendous character where three large and notable buildings are seen in swiftly changing relation in a distance of no more than some forty or fifty yards. This happens alongside the short straight pavement on the east side of Catte Street in the central part of the University area.

MOVING CAMERA

At the northern end of Catte Street, by its junction with New College Lane, the only building to be seen on the west

45

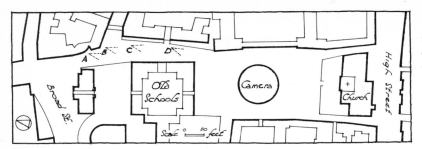

Oxford. Plan of Catte Street, with view points marked as A; B; C; D.

Catte St., view from A.

side is the noble cube of the old Bodleian. Advancing some ten yards or so along the pavement, one sees coming into view the first tentative beginnings of the rotunda of the Radcliffe Camera and the upper spire of the University Church. Ten more yards and something like a third of the rotunda and dome, and half the church tower, are in view. Ten more

Catte St., view from B.

and the Camera is half out from the angle of the Bodleian
walls. Ten more again and the vast bulk of rotunda and
dome has emerged, has separated from the Bodleian, and
stands free against the surrounding sky – as, in a few yards
again, does the tower of the church beyond. Cube, cylinder,
cone, the pure primal elemental forms are suddenly juxta-

Catte St., view from C.

posed; or, rather, with a rapidity that is almost suddenness, deploy out from each other in a series of effects that is architecturally sensational; a series of effects that illustrates, in very essence, the characteristic quality of the kinetic attribute.

Catte St., view from D.

Town and townscape

HIGH STREET

Having savoured these essences of townscape in this small space in Catte Street and its neighbourhood, we can now proceed to take more prolonged draughts of it in other streets in Oxford. And we may as well begin with what is, beyond doubt, one of the finest pieces of sustained townscape in the world, namely High Street.

There are four main variations of this townscape (as of most) – two on each side of the street. Indeed in a very wide street there may be many minor, but still telling, variations besides. One's position on a broad pavement, whether one is close in to the walling buildings, at one or more points towards the middle of the pavement, or at its edge, can give strikingly varying effects of progression and unfolding. High Street is wide enough to provide some of these additional variations. For our purpose here we look at the two westward and the two eastward unfoldings in the middle of each pavement. This is something that probably not many people have done or will do deliberately, for it requires a two-mile walk. But it is a revealing multiplication of a moving experience to take them at a single enterprise – a kind of townscape progress in four reels.

It must be acknowledged at once that the north side of the street is more important, architecturally, than the south side. That it is the concave side of the curve would, in any case, make it so, especially since it faces south and the sun. But, with singular happiness, it is on this side, where they can best be seen, that the finest buildings, and those which create the most telling effects, occur.

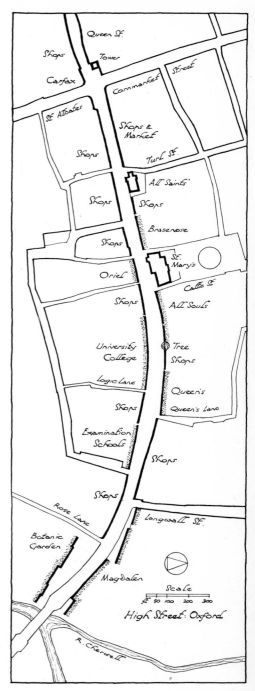

Oxford. Plan of the frontages of High Street, showing the intermixture of town and university buildings.

Oxford. The beginning of High Street, seen above the traffic, looking east: shops, the tower of All Saints Church, with the spire of St Mary's (the University Church) behind.

51

Town and townscape

From Carfax eastward on the south side

From the south-side pavement at Carfax, the great street ranges down in full perspective for half its total eastward length. It is a scene which is nobly composed and admirably diversified. Beyond the first range of shops, the black-and-white western bit of the large store there charmingly foils the predominant stone. The rest of the store beyond, somewhat lower than the adjoining buildings and smoothly composed with a central pediment over its regular ashlar, is in marked contrast to its boxy neighbour, the Mitre Hotel, whose stepped frontage provides a base, in this view, for the tower and spire of All Saints. And here, in this view of All Saints, the City Church, there is an unusual effect – to find for once in Oxford, a monumental university building subordinated to a monumental city building, in the way the upper part of the spire of the near-by St Mary's (the University Church) seems to stand modestly and even solicitously beside and below the All Saints spire, as though preparing to slip into hiding behind it. All this, with the Brasenose and All Souls frontages on the street line stretching away down to where the first pavilion-like pedimented gable of Queen's comes forward beyond the green roundness of the sycamore which leans out as a marvellous foil from All Souls – all this is perhaps the most concentrated and lively street-scene in the city.

The street-scene becomes the townscape as one moves on and the buildings begin to deploy. As the tower of the City Church grows gigantic and passes behind, St Mary's spire seems to drop down and come forward till it rises directly and curiously out of the tower of Brasenose's little-used Jackson gateway. A yard or two farther on, the Queen's buildings have disappeared round the curve, though the Tree continues to occupy the centre of the picture straight ahead; and in the foreground the enrichments of the lower spire of St Mary's rise now out of Brasenose gables, while its twisted barley-sugar porch columns (Oxford's one bit of full-blooded baroque) and the pinnacled wall of its nave, based on bushes, have stepped forward into the now narrowed view.

By Oriel's frontage as one starts to round the bend,

High Street, by All Souls, looking eastward t Queen's. The sycamore leaning out into the stree at the central point on the concave side of the curve plays an immensely important part in High Street's townscape, foiling the buildings and introducing a special point of punctuation in a vital position.

Queen's comes in again, and the view begins to open out
progressively. Now that one is nearer them, the foiling quality
of the four uneven-heighted and uneven-fronted shops between All Souls and Queen's can be appreciated. Beyond
Queen's, rounding the curve, there are more of them, until,
towards the end of University College frontage, just before
Logic Lane, the gables and pinnacles of the first Magdalen
buildings begin to show above another and a different foil,
a group of service trees, now of recent years grown so big
as to begin to endanger the view altogether.

Again, for a while, the view becomes near-static. Then,
by Merton Street, just as the possible range of interplay
between forms in perspective seems to be running out after
the long progress down the street, there comes the perfect
interpolation for the occasion – the gabled west end of
Magdalen chapel, with its great window, seen in dead-eleva-
tion. And now the street ends with a perfectly timed and

53

perfectly sustained climax. Beyond the far side, the trees of Magdalen Grove have moved into view – such a number of them, this time, to act, not as a foil, but as the indication of an end. A further low line of Magdalen buildings has also come in, along the far frontage. And slowly, impressively, Magdalen's noble tower moves in from the wall of buildings

High Street, looking east, by Queen's. Shops stretching down to where Magdalen Chapel is just beginning to come out into the scene.

backing this southern pavement, until, just before Rose Lane is reached, it disengages, separates, stands erect in an increasing space of sky in the middle of the view, its base lightly barred by the tree rising from the corner of the garden of Magdalen Gate House.

It would be better to end here; for, a few yards beyond, murder was done some years ago – townscape murder. Originally, at the back of this south-side pavement, along the edge of the grass-banked forecourt to the Botanic Garden, a single row of limes gave a rounded foil to the tower – and beyond them, alongside Magdalen Bridge, a row of Lombardy poplars foiled the foil by slimly reasserting, in the background, the tower's verticality – making a complicated and subtle scene. But now the limes have gone and the poplars have been so truncated that their vertical punctuation has been lost. Even more disastrously the greensward, which made a contribution to High Street townscape that

Magdalen Tower, the culminating feature in the eastward view down High Street, as the concluding part of the street's curve brings it out from the buildings on the right and stands it powerfully in the middle of the scene.

was invaluable in its simplicity of means, has been exchanged for an umbrageous mess of plottage. It had provided a vivid termination and beginning for High Street – for the eastward direction an opening out, a nicely measured explosion of space between the end of the long canalized unfolding and then the narrowing of space again in the slow balustraded rise of Magdalen Bridge: for the other direction a preparation, a moment of pause, before the great progression began. But then the second or third wealthiest college in Oxford, dripping with endowments, snatched at the offer of a few thousand pounds by an alien lady whose god-wot eyes couldn't bear the thought of Oxford without a rose garden, and made in place of the simple grass the kind of small-scaled box-edged multi-plotted rose-and-pleached-beech parterre that might have been successful for a minor Cotswold manor-house but whose vulgarity in Oxford High Street only seems to show the sad corruption into triviality that can happen where there is no understanding. Whether the Fellows of Magdalen can ever be persuaded to sweep their derogatory nonsense away and clear the ground again may be open to doubt. But in the meanwhile the only *townscape* reason for going beyond Rose Lane is to get a proper beginning for the westward progress, the return perambulation along High Street.

From Magdalen westward on the north side

While the eastward perambulation began with a highly concentrated street-scene, this westward one begins with the opposite kind of effect. At the middle of Magdalen Bridge the view northwards is along the tree-folded valley of the Cherwell, beyond the fritillary meadows, with not a building to be seen – and in the foreground the enchanting smooth greenness of Angel Meadow enables one to appreciate what an eighteenth-century poet meant when he spoke of 'the enamelled turf'. Ahead, looking straight up High Street to avoid as far as one can that mad and muddled garden on the left, the scene is of low buildings stretching away from the great vertical punctuation of the tower, as it rises immense beyond an ilex that is rooted below the bridge. As one moves forward, the scene at the beginning is near-static, with a slow

High Street: the early part of the westward progress: shops, Queen's, with the dome of the Radcliffe Camera topping it beyond.

56

unfolding of the commercial buildings just beyond the
Longwall Street junction. Then, a hundred yards farther on,
by Magdalen porter's lodge where the road begins to curve,
the eastern wing of Queen's, then the cupola, come suddenly in. Half a dozen yards more, and the immense grey-
black dome of the Radcliffe Camera (a building which we
did not see at all on the eastward perambulation) is seen
rising with Roman effect above Queen's western wing, which
has also moved into view. A dozen yards again, and *there* is
the Tree. In the next dozen, the All Souls frontage has un-
folded itself, and first the spire of St Mary's and then its
tower base have disengaged themselves from the south-side
buildings at the head of the curve and have stood forward
into the sky.

57

Looking west by
Queen's, where the curve
in the street has brought
St Mary's spired tower
out from behind the
southern-side buildings
and has stood it
majestically against the
sky.

Here in these hundred yards between Magdalen lodge and
Longwall Street is a piece of townscape as dramatic as that of
Catte Street itself – and nearly as tremendous. It could hardly
be expected to continue at that pitch: and it does not. For a
short while, as one goes forward, there is a quieter period.
The Queen's cupola and gables, the Tree, the low-looking
buildings of All Souls, and St Mary's spire, all deploy and
resolve gently about, the spire moving slowly into the centre
of the view, its lower pinnacles fretted against the sky. Then,
just beyond Queen's Lane, the drama is renewed as the spire
of All Saints and Brasenose gate-tower seem, because of some
quirk on the opposite frontage, to sail out *suddenly* into the
picture, so that there are now *two* well-spaced spires of almost
equal height rising into the sky. By Queen's gateway, the

A few yards farther on, another spire, All Saints, has moved dramatically in from the southern side. Now the scene is splendidly rich and moving; the sweeping curve; Queen's western pavilion; a few shops; the sycamore (here in winter bareness); All Souls frontage; St Mary's spire and fretted nave; Brasenose frontage and gateway tower, with All Saints tower beyond.

tower of St Mary's, but not the spire, has disappeared behind the Tree. A few yards farther, Carfax tower has appeared. And now one gets again, as in Catte Street, an interplay between the elemental forms, though here with a quite different and piquant rather than a grand effect, as the cone of St Mary's, the cylinder of All Saints, and the cube of Carfax stand against the sky at nearly equal distances.

By the Tree, St Mary's spire has gone from the view; and, beyond the pinnacled nave, All Saints is left in possession of the sky, inseparably related (as in all views of this part of the street) to Brasenose gateway, and sometimes apparently attached to it; while, beyond, the Carfax tower seems to sit at its feet. But in spite of these and other changing effects, something of the life has gone out of this westward perambulation by the time Catte Street is reached. The drama has been too strong to be sustained. Still, if it lacks the climax of the eastern progress, it also avoids the anticlimax of that awful garden. And though it has now become something of a set-scene rather than an unfolding, by any other standards than Oxford's highest this is still exceptional townscape – and, moreover, it will provide the pot of tea or the cup of coffee which may be necessary to encourage the undertaking of the two remaining reels of this kinetic progress.

East on the north: west on the south

Descriptions pall. So it may be better merely to mention briefly the more special effects in the remaining variations of this High Street townscape rather than describe the full progressions about it.

The eastward perambulation on the north side begins with a major loss, for one is too close under the two churches for the spire of either of them to be visible; and though the Tree and the first gable and cupola of Queen's can be seen from the beginning, the rest of the north-side buildings as far down as that are merely a framing wall. Because of that, this is the least effective of the four beginnings. But the middle and final sequences, at least, have the fine movement that is the great street's characteristic. By the gateway to All Souls the first Magdalen buildings come in beyond the north-side shops: and soon the great window of the chapel is at the head of the street. Then, just before Queen's gateway, the pinnacled top of Magdalen tower rises over the gables of the east end of the Examination Schools on the opposite side, and, because of the jut of the street at Eastgate, it stays above the roofs for a long time, its full length beginning to come in only as one gets opposite the Schools' entrance, and not being wholly disengaged until just before Longwall Street – a preparation and a slow unfolding for a sudden climax that is perfect of its kind.

As the beginnings of the westward perambulation on the north side were dramatic, so they are on the south. At Rose Lane the first parts of Queen's begin to move in; and within a few yards, opposite Longwall Street, they are all in the picture, with the grey dome of the Camera above them and the Tree beyond. In a few more yards, by Merton Street, the

High Street's end, looking west: All Saints porch; hotel; shops; and Carfax tower.

61

dome has almost (but not quite) gone out of view beyond some unusually fat Queen's chimneys in the foreground; but it suddenly begins to emerge again, seen above domestic buildings by the entrance to the Schools, grown big and immensely powerful in the meanwhile. Here also, as on the other side, the spires of the two churches seem to emerge and detach themselves from the southern walls quite suddenly; and the spire of All Saints makes another of its curious attachments to Brasenose gate-tower. And in its ending this south-side progress is more satisfactory than that on the north, for though Carfax tower remains somewhat inadequate for a full climax, at least the view is closed and Queen Street's somewhat indeterminate slit of sky is absent, while the lively urbanity of the architectural sequence of All Saints, the Mitre and the shops beyond, is full of the character of fine townscape.

SUDDEN ENTRIES

These, then, are some of the effects to be seen in four perambulations along the pavements of Oxford's High Street. They are rich and dramatic enough. But some of the most dramatic revelations of the street's grandeur do not belong to perambulations within its own confines. These additional excitements arise by sudden entries into it from narrow side streets. The debouchments from the narrow slits of the Markets, from Catte Street, Turl Street, Queen's Lane, Alfred Street, Oriel Street and Logic Lane, and even from the wider openings of Longwall, King Edward Street and Merton Street, are all of a suddenly revealing kind: and so are the entrances from colleges (All Souls, Queen's, Magdalen, Oriel and University) and indeed from any shop or other building lining the street. Perhaps the most dramatic of them all is that vouchsafed at the end of Queen's Lane. Here after a long narrow walled-in passage that for the most part lacks striking incident (though by way of contrast with the rest of the city streets it has a quality of secrecy that is all its own) – here the debouchment occurs at the very heart of the great street, at the very point of its perfection; and, particularly in the first, the westward, view, it occurs like a burst of great music on unexpectant ears.

Oxford air-view. The contrast between the confined irregular character of the streets and the more open and regular character of the college quadrangles furth, enriches the city's townscape.

62

It is of sudden dramatic effects like these, as well as in the more gradual unfoldings and the kinetic progressions, that the many-faceted pleasures of townscape are compounded.

COLLEGIATE IN-AND-OUT

While High Street is its chief glory, the remarkable thing about Oxford's townscape, the attribute which places it so high among the townscapes of the world, is the largeness and continuity of its extent, the way fine qualities characterize almost every part of the central area of the city. The rest of the main streets and the smaller streets cannot, of course, approach High Street's and Catte Street's near perfection; and in some of them kinetic character diminishes towards the near-static. But almost all of them have a character and a quality that elsewhere would give them outstanding distinction in their own right: and their concentration and continuity here, with hardly a major deficiency among them (though, of course, inevitably with faults and blemishes in various degrees) constitute something which, after a hundred years of urban chaos, seems little short of miraculous – miraculous not only that it has survived but that it was ever achieved at all.

But beside the public townscape of the streets there is in Oxford an addition which extends it in a most enriching way. That addition is provided by the colleges in the relationship, the interplay, between the form and character of the streets and the form and character of the building complexes behind them. In most towns such complexes, in so far as they now exist at all, may generally not be available for wide public enjoyment, and may be experienced only by those having right or need to use the buildings comprising them – though this is no reason why, if such a relationship of internal complexes to external streets does indeed provide such townscape enrichments, it should not be more employed in future planning and building. Oxford, as a university city, is, of course, a very special example of this kind of townscape extension; and a glance at some of its unusual richness in this respect may not only provide its own pleasures but may serve to establish some principles as to what similar (if necessarily less extensive) effects might, in the future, be gained elsewhere.

Oxford colleges (and there are nearly forty of them within the University) are not only largely autonomous, they are physically self-contained and quite firmly separated from each other even in the instances where their sites and buildings are adjacent and adjoined. Except in one or two instances, it is not possible to walk through a college and its grounds and come out at another place. Nor is it possible to walk out of one college into another. You have to go in from the public street, under the arch of the college gateway, past the porter's lodge, and out again into the public street at the place where you came in. So there is no possibility of progressing from one set of academic scenes to another. You must always come back to the wider public setting. And in this way you get a most vital interplay of visual experience between the academic and the public parts of the city: you

Oxford. The 'dreaming spires' skyline. A single high tower-building in the modern fashion could entirely shatter all this. One, higher than anything seen here, was recently proposed (but fortunately rejected) beyond the buildings on the left side of the view.

64

get a moving interplay of environmental and architectural relationship.

The interplay is, of course, in the space-relationships, in the plan-forms, as well as in the architecture. And it operates initially within each college itself, as well as between each college and the city outside. The college buildings are arranged in a succession of courts or quadrangles ('quads' in the Oxford vernacular) – and since there are two or three quads to every college there must be something approaching a hundred of them in Oxford. Because these were built at various times and to varying sizes they have a very varying architectural character. Thus not only each college but each quad within each college has its own individuality, and its own sense of being a separate and generally a fully enclosed place. Moreover, the links between the different quads in each college are often reticent and to unfamiliar eyes obscure, the passage from one to another being often made by a narrow tunnel-opening apparently informally placed. So, even within each college there is almost always visual variety and contrast – and sometimes architectural drama as well.

But there is more than that. The contrast and drama between the internal collegiate scenes and those of the city outside are again different in kind and extent. Whether they are wide or narrow, comparatively straight or markedly curving, the streets, in their elongated and flowing configuration are dramatically different from the squarer, more regular, more finite and enclosed forms of the quads. Moving through a college gateway, inward from street to quad, or outward from quad to street, is to experience a vivid visual contrast, a strong sense of environmental change, a change almost to a different kind of physical world. And this feeling is, of course, strengthened by the quietness of the quads and gardens in contrast to the loud busyness of the streets outside.

In a sense this kind of visual experience is somewhat special, even in Oxford, in that it is not one that inevitably even if subconsciously must occur to the ordinary citizen as he passes on his ordinary purposes about the city. The college inhabitant, the deliberate sight-seer, experiences it; but not the ordinary man literally in the street. Nevertheless, this private extension of the public townscape – private though readily accessible to the public through the generosity of its owners – is an indivisible part of the total townscape of Oxford.

It occasionally is so in other places. Certainly it is in most cathedral-cities (or would be if the cathedral authorities did not allow their closes to be betrayed for the pieces of silver that can be extracted from motorists). And so it is in other cities with universities or large institutions of one kind or another. It is naturally not common in the general run of towns, because it is a condition which only uncommon functions in the past have called into being. Yet its contribution to a town's amenities is so great that one could wish that it might be sought after and achieved in other places and in other ways. Without doubt it could be got even in ordinary towns if plans were made for it. The now not-unusual constitution of 'pedestrian shopping-precincts' could be adapted to establish such effects. So no doubt could the arrangement of public buildings in association. Or groups of office buildings. Or of central-city living quarters. Or of other facilities.

Certainly this Oxford relationship of the townscape of the public streets and of private places contributes in no small measure to the visual pleasures of that richly endowed city.

66

V   AND OTHER TOWNS

We have observed Oxford in some detail because it is the pre-eminent example of townscape in Britain. But in our initial consideration of the conception of townscape as a way of looking at our towns, the point was made that it is an experience that can be gained in almost any town. To repeat what was said earlier:

> the appreciation and enjoyment of townscape as such is not in the least limited to places where good architecture exists, nor to those who have expert eyes to see it. It is a pleasure to be got in any town that has some interest of form: and it can be enjoyed by anyone who cares to enjoy it.

So, even at the risk of indulging in a surfeit of description, it may be useful for the purposes of demonstration to cast a further rapid eye on a few other places of varying size and character.

CAPITAL CITY

London in its vastness has so many thousand townscape variations that it may be invidious to attempt to choose one or two by way of illustration. But two particular major examples may be taken because after so much praise of one total townscape it may be useful to cite effects in another that are less successful, and because both provide sad lessons of the fate that can overtake even famous places through insensitive and ill-considered new building. They are Whitehall and the Ludgate Hill approach to St Paul's.

Whitehall is rather like a big brother to Oxford High Street. It has the same slow curve. It has a splendidly placed group of trees about the central point on the concave side.

67

And if it somewhat lacks, in parts, some foiling admixture of other than government buildings, it has two main attributes that save it from oppressive monumentality – the two breaks in over-similar continuity which occur in the drop of building height at the screens at the Horse Guards and at the Admiralty, and in the recession on the opposite side, where the trees are.

That is how it was until a year or two ago: the government centre of a capital city which, in the way of most English towns, had managed, even at this level of large building, to maintain a human scale. It avoided the pomposity that is so often associated with governmental precincts elsewhere. It possessed form without formality, dignity without display. There was no one building extravagantly overtopping the rest. Even the Houses of Parliament themselves stood unassertive, with only the Victoria Tower rising moderately into the sky on one side of the southward view. It was a civilized, freely ordered, slowly unfolding broad street of just a proper measure of nobility. It was admirably complete, admirably right for its purpose. It was a piece of townscape of great distinction, modest grandeur, continuing interest. And now? Now it is ruined. It has been shattered, incidentally, accidentally, blindly, without a thought given to it: shattered by the distant addition that now rears up into its opening of western sky – the monstrous tower, not of some new government building (though it has become partly occupied by government offices) but of a private commercial company that has been permitted to dominate the ordered place of government itself – an outrage which more properly belongs to the consideration which we shall have to make later of the whole matter of towers in townscape, but which it would be perverse not to mention here and now.

The other example in London townscape is the approach to St Paul's up Ludgate Hill. It is oblique in direction with only one lopsided view of an incomplete feature of the Cathedral's façade visible, the full view not opening out until the spectator is almost too near to see it as a whole. That arrangement (if it can be called such) has long been the subject of argument. There are those who maintain that the

London: a private tower of offices leaps up and usurps domination of the government centre in Whitehall.

69

approach to so massive a building, especially since it is a
great national shrine, should be as direct, as spectacular, as
monumental as the building itself; and that the sidelong hit-
and-miss approach is unhappy and unworthy. There are
others who rationalize an unsatisfactory result by reference
to those informal conditions that so often elsewhere produce
the effects of drama – delayed climax, sudden revelation and
so on – which, as we have seen, by way of Oxford, are among
the special attributes of great townscape.

The plain fact is that this approach to St Paul's has never
been either one thing or the other. To rectify the unsatisfactory effect was bound to be difficult – so difficult that it
might have been better not to attempt it save in the most
thoroughgoing way. Certainly what has been done has been
extraordinarily mistaken. Where before the alignment of the
top of the street was wrong by accident it is now wrong by
design. Before, the street more or less ignored the Cathedral.
Now, the side which blocks the view has been widened out
towards the top of the rise as the building is approached – a
widening that could have no purpose or justification but to
suggest the preparation for an opening out of the view. And
then, where after that preparation the view should open out,
it is deliberately denied by the thrusting forward of a building
to shut it away. This recent 'improvement' to the approach to
St Paul's is a lesson to show that in townscape, as in all else,
frustration stultifies whereas measured delay need not.

CATHEDRAL CITY

If St Paul's is an example of a formal building unsatis-
factorily related to its informal setting, almost all medieval
cathedrals carry some visual excitement in their relationship
to their street approaches. Canterbury, Durham and York
may be taken as differing examples to show how various
these relationships may be.

Canterbury has an example of what may be called the 'barred
approach'. The way to the Cathedral off the long High Street
is by the short, narrow, faintly curving Mercery Lane. The
view down it is simply a piling-up and recession of building-
planes – first the irregularly overhung street itself framing the

*London: Ludgate Hill
and St Paul's. Designed
frustration. The street
has been widened as
though to provide an
extended view of the
Cathedral, then a new
building is deliberately
thrust forward to shut it
out.*

70

Town and townscape

narrow view; then a stone gateway placed powerfully across the end of it rather higher than the approaching buildings; and away beyond that, through the arch of the gateway, only some flanking buildings and the solid lower wall of the great church faintly visible, with the crowding pinnacles of its western towers rising above the gateway. As one advances along the street the towers seem to lower themselves, until, near the gateway, they have dropped out of sight (and here a delaying subsidiary effect, unperceived in the earlier part of the approach, has come into being in the miniscule market-place that is almost wholly taken up by its little market-building). Through the shadowed archway, a step into the Close. And there the great Cathedral – not only the towers that have previously declared themselves and then retired, not only they but the whole length and height of it – stands massively before one's eyes.

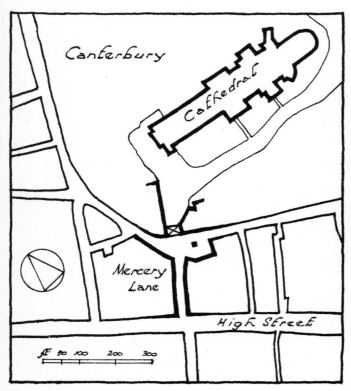

LEFT

*At the end of the street,
by a miniscule market-
place, the Cathedral's
pinnacles have dropped
down behind the gatehouse,
and only a glimpse of its
porch is to be seen among
a perspective of domestic
buildings.*

RIGHT

*Out from the archway of
the gatehouse, the western
towers, the nave and the
central tower of the
Cathedral are dramatic-
ally revealed.*

Durham is an example of another kind of approach: the
approach with a delayed but unbarred climax. From a narrow
street rising out of the high market-place (itself an admirable
long length of slowly unfolding townscape), another narrow
street, Owengate, leading off, discloses a glimpse of towers.
As one climbs up it, steep and curving, the view of the towers
at first changes little until, at the top of the rise, at the head
of the curve, the confined view having thus far excited one's
feelings of mystery and expectation, the street suddenly
debouches into a large elevated square with a wide expanse
of sky, the whole of the great Cathedral – not merely the
western towers that hitherto occupied the view, but nave,
central tower, chancel, ambulatory, eastern pinnacles –
majestically occupying all the facing side of it.

And here in this Durham example of kinetic townscape
is an example of something else – of its survival against

consolidated odds. It is the character and alignment of the buildings on the concave side of the curve of Owengate, as much as the alignment of the street itself, that contributes to the total effect. But a year or two ago the University was determined to demolish them. It wanted in their place a collection of nice minimum bedsitters for students. The first design for the new buildings was in thin neo-Georgian to an alignment that had nothing to do with the alignment that contributed

Durham. The approach to the Cathedral has the qualities of mystery and revelation. From the Market Place (plan, page 76), a narrow climbing street slowly curving away into the distance; a short rising swiftly-curving street taking off on the right, with a glimpse of towers across a vague intermediate distance beyond.

so much to the effect – that, indeed, largely destroyed it. After months of argument, that was rejected by the planning powers. Even they were divided among themselves. One rejected it because it was all for demolition but wanted glassy modern instead of neo-Georgian architecture. The other took its whole stand on the principle of let-well-alone. A distinguished architect-surveyor brought in by the University said the buildings couldn't be saved, weren't worth saving,

Progressing up the street, the towers come more closely into view with the rest of the building still obscured until, at the top of the rise, it all stands suddenly revealed beyond a great hill-top square in a wide expanse of sky.

Town and townscape

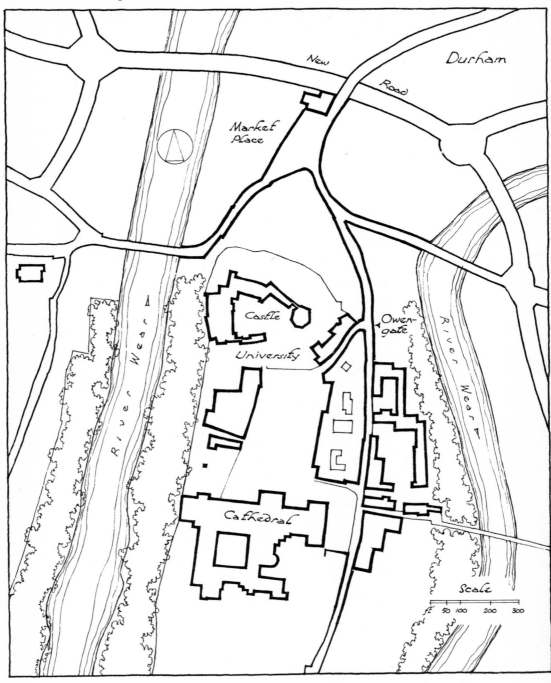

and might fall down any minute. Societies for the protection of ancient buildings refused to be interested. The Ministry responsible for old buildings shut its eyes. The University's determination continued. All seemed lost. Only a last agonized appeal by the let-well-alone camp, threats of exposure for philistinism, and the nomination of an architect who would save the street and adapt it to university needs, at last prevailed. And so in the end the street was preserved and rehabilitated; and not only was the townscape saved by the narrowest squeak but in the saving the University got all the accommodation it would have achieved through destruction, and at half the cost.

And here at Durham another narrow squeak may be recorded. In this small two-storey town, a year or two ago, the Post Office proposed to put up a sixteen-storey tower of offices. The County Council (the statutory planning authority) excitedly welcomed the idea. But the town's adviser privately persuaded the Post Office architects to omit the tower and build to a more acceptable height – an achievement which saved the town but, sadly for him, lost him his job.

York provides townscape effects different again from these at Canterbury and Durham. And in at least one of them it shows the success that is so badly lacking in that view of St Paul's up Ludgate Hill. There, looking along Low Petergate, the towers of the Cathedral rise beyond intervening buildings to make a most richly complicated scene which the curve of the street itself, in its slow variation and unfolding, still further enriches, while the obscurity of the approach to the towering building has added to it a kind of beckoning invitation that is very different from the sense of frustration that the newly designed approach to St Paul's induces.

PROVINCIAL CITY

Many of the large provincial cities have cathedrals too; but that does not make them cathedral-cities in the sense in which that term is ordinarily understood, any more than the possession of a university makes them university-cities. Manchester, Liverpool, Birmingham and the rest are like

*urham. The situation of
e Cathedral: plan.

77

York. The Cathedral as a delayed climax beyond the end of the street. In the street itself a modern building not strikingly disharmonious in design.

RVY 36

London in their possession of so many variations of townscape that it would be invidious to choose one or two by way of illustration. So instead of attempting to make such a choice it may be better to take two examples of a special kind

– two instances of deliberately contrived rather than the more usual 'natural-grown' townscape.

Newcastle upon Tyne provides an excellent example of that in the extensive central-city area which was redeveloped there in the 1830s. Beyond the first steep crowded banks of the Tyne, Grey Street, wide, regular, fronted by stepped classical façades, flows up in a sweeping curve to a classical column in the heart of the city's somewhat disarrayed shopping centre. It is a beautifully modelled, smooth, regular and generous progression, which, even without special elements, would be striking both in its own quality of slow unfolding and in its contrast to the rest of the city streets outside the redeveloped area. But in addition to those general attributes it has two features which, together with the culminating column, contribute most strikingly to the total effect. One, a subtle

Newcastle upon Tyne. Grey Street, the principal street of this fine example of town planning. A long rising curve, a monumental column as a terminal feature at the head, small domes on the topmost building on the concave side, a theatre's great portico stepping into the street to give a strong point of emphasis on the convex side.

Newcastle upon Tyne. Eldon Square, the only square in the great planned extension of the city in the 1830s: acquired now for demolition by the City Council, the authority specifically charged with the responsibility of safeguarding the city's architectural character.

apparently trivial addition, is the way the small domes of the arcade towards the top of the concave side of the street provide just the right points of punctuation there. The other, altogether larger in scale and outstanding in fact and effect, is the way the portico of the Theatre Royal steps forward over the pavement on the opposite side at a vital position a little lower down – a notable and unusual instance of a major enrichment to townscape provided on the *convex* and generally less contributory side of a curving street. (But here again, as at Durham, threatened disaster must be recorded, for the City Council has deliberately bought up its second finest example of monumental planning, the noble quadrangle of Eldon Square, for the sole purpose of demolishing it – a most blind and bitter action by the very authority itself which is charged with the conservation of the city's character and buildings.)

Bristol. A tower of 1925 finely placed at a change of direction of a steeply rising street.

And other towns

Bristol, like Newcastle, also provides an example of a key building in a curving upward view. There, at the vital change of direction of Park Street and Queen's Road, the tower of the Wills Memorial Hall of the University seems to step forward into the middle of the scene, to vitalize and diversify it with powerful effect – an effect of major importance in the city, and one created as recently as 1925.

Town and townscape

But in spite of all the multitudinous instances of good and even splendid townscape in the larger towns and cities, it is the country towns of England that, next to the university-cities and the cathedral-cities, show it in greatest richness.

Stamford does so pre-eminently. On the Northampton border of Lincolnshire, it is the finest town of its size, and one of the finest of any size, anywhere in Britain. A mere country town (pop. *c.* 12,000), without cathedral, university[1] or any such character-giving institution, its stone-built streets have an air of sophistication and urbanity that a country town does not ordinarily possess. It has altogether unusual distinction in the sheer quantity of its good architecture, and in its no less than five spired or towered parish churches a mere hundred yards apart. But it is the way these compose into townscape on its striking street forms that make it the truly remarkable place that it is. In spite of the by-pass that now diverts much traffic into the adjoining countryside, it is still a town that suffers severely from vehicles: and it is to be hoped that some day soon it may be relieved of most of these as well. In the meanwhile, taking care as one moves along its streets, there is here one of the most rapidly dramatic townscapes of any town in Britain to be enjoyed.

Entering from the south, the town begins immediately in solid eighteenth-century buildings at the end of the park wall of Burleigh House. There are no suburbs here: after country suddenly it is town. The handsome street, with the square tower of St Martin's Church on the convex side, flows down in a slow double curve to the Welland Bridge. From the bridge there is a wide town panorama, with, at the top of the short sharply rising street immediately ahead, the great tower and steeple of St Mary's Church mightily dominating all; and, to the left, strong horizontal lines of buildings rising beyond the river, with the tower of St John's and the spire of All Saints riding over their roofs. Up St Mary's Hill ahead

---

[1] Though it did possess a kind of one once when Brasenose absented itself there from Oxford in 1334 with such effect that for 500 years Oxford graduates were forced to take an oath to have nothing to do with the rival establishment at Stamford, even though it had long passed out of existence.

Stamford, Lincs. The great tower and steeple of St Mary's Church on a short hill beyond the bridge-head at the entrance to the inner town.

(fine public buildings and the recession of a small square on the right), at the T-junction where the great tower steps forward, one part of St Mary's Street quickly curves away beyond a jutting building on the right, and the level main-street part of it dog-legs sharply to the left. A hundred yards more, and it dog-legs to the right (the Sheep Market square a little ahead and below being hidden). Then it gives a short leap again with the square tower of St John's on the right, and gabled buildings closing the view beyond. At the church tower, Red Lion Square suddenly opens out with most of

Town and townscape

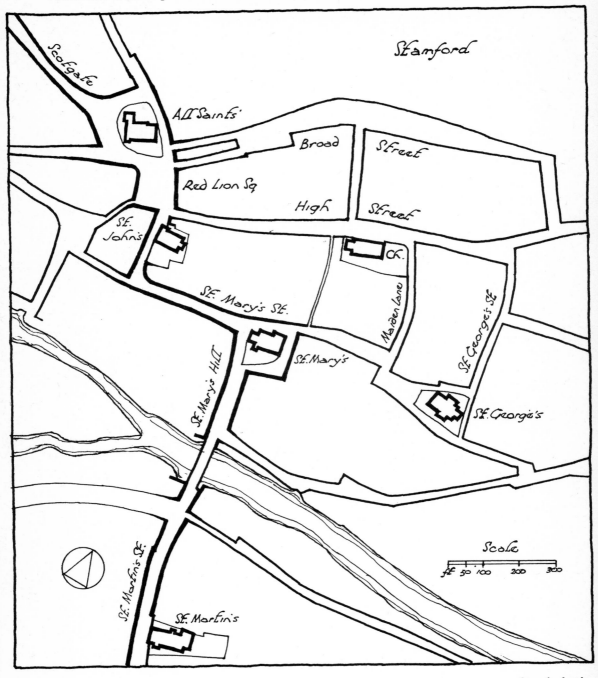

Stamford: plan.

*The main street turns
sharply left at the church:
a local street curves off to
the right.*

the facing side taken up by All Saints, high-spired and
narrowly islanded by cobbled streets. Round two sides of the
square, a dog-leg to the right past the church leads out of the
town by another narrow curving (and more commonplace)
street, Scotgate. All this, from the bridge onwards, in five
hundred yards.

Southwards the return progress by the main-road streets
creates, as usual, a series of different effects. From Scotgate,
the view is of the great west window and the spire of All

Winding street, with spire and steeple of two churches which are themselves obscured by the street's buildings.

Saints, with the tower of St John's and the steeple of St Mary's over the roofs of the square. A dog-leg into the square discloses the whole of St John's at the far angle and the steeple of St Mary's right in the centre of the picture (and in the other angle a thirty-yard gunnel into Sheep Market). At the angle by St John's, High Street is glimpsed curving away, with still another church tower rising beyond its roofs. Ahead, at the bottom of St John's Street, the woods of Burleigh House rise distantly above the low buildings. The sharp turn to the left into St Mary's Street brings in the tower-and-spire hugely dominating the first part of the street,

86

while the rest proceeds obscurely out beyond it. To the right at the church, with St Mary's Place opening out in fine buildings and a tree or two, the street drops steeply down to Welland Bridge, and curves out of the town beyond it.

Those are the main-road progresses. There are other, less traffic-harassed ones, in the town that lies eastward of those streets. There is High Street, comparatively level, on a long slow double curve, with many handsome eighteenth- and early nineteenth-century frontages above its mostly modern shops, and in its middle part the church whose tower we distantly glimpsed from Red Lion Square. There is Broad Street, curving, narrowing again and dog-legging out of sight, with many good eighteenth-century buildings mostly on the concave and sunlit side. And as well as these, there are

The way out from the central part of the town.

Town and townscape

contrasting minor streets; Ironmonger Street with its downward view to the church tower; St George's Street and Maiden Lane, both narrow curving and falling to where St George's Church fronts its small square; Cheyne Lane, a curving pedestrian gunnel with shops; the cobbled street round All Saints; and others besides.

King's Lynn in Norfolk is different again. Although it is a port its plan-form makes little acknowledgement of the fact, except that some of its streets, wholly obscured from the river-shore, run parallel to it. One of them, the main shopping street, is an illustration of what has earlier been said – that even the drabbest street can hold the interest of the spectator if by virtue of its alignment it possesses some kinetic quality. Architecturally High Street is of the most commonplace kind: indeed most of its buildings are characterless and some are brutally offensive: yet because throughout its extremely narrow length it takes a long curving form it has

King's Lynn, Norfolk. Nelson Street, the entrance from the south.

*St Margaret's Church
and the approach to
Saturday Market Place.*

qualities of unfolding and containment that not only reduce
its dullness but provoke and sustain some visual interest as
well. But if this street is otherwise commonplace, the street-
sequence nearer the shore is altogether outstanding both in
its architecture and in its townscape. It begins in a crooked
little street of old houses by a small river inlet; passes through
a roughly triangular *place* (Saturday Market Place) where the
fine parish church and the chequer-fronted Guildhall are;
leaves it by an obscure corner exit; as Queen Street twists
narrowly by elegantly-fronted seventeenth-century merchant-
houses; dog-legs by a bridge over another inlet fronted by a
splendid seventeenth-century Customs House; proceeds by
the somewhat wider and more gently curving King Street of
similarly distinguished houses; and emerges into a great
space (Tuesday Market Place) with the strong spire of the
hidden St Nicholas' Church, beyond one corner, overtopping
the fine country-town commercial buildings that enclose it –
enclose it so firmly and continuously that to the unfamiliar
eye there is apparently no way out. Here in this sequence of

89

*Past the fine Customs
House, after narrow
twisting Queen Street,
King Street broadens a
little with a more gentle
curve and is lined with
merchants' houses.*

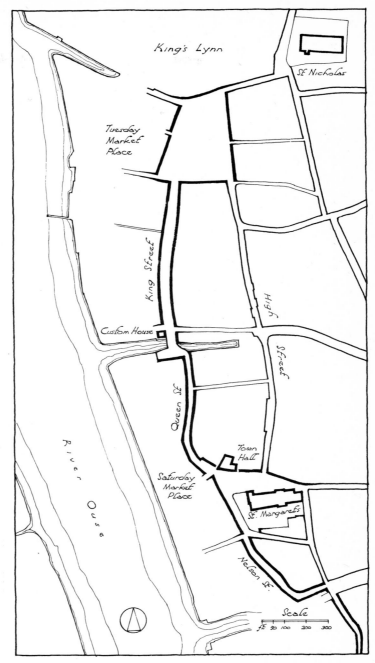

*King Street opens
suddenly into the wide
Tuesday Market Place,
lined with solid country-
town commercial buildings,
and with the spire of the
unseen St Nicholas' Church
rising beyond a corner of it.*

91

King's Lynn, Norfolk:
plan.

streets and *places* there is a sustained continuity of unfolding townscape which is not unworthy of being mentioned alongside that of Stamford itself.

Richmond in Yorkshire is different from Stamford and King's Lynn in its concentration of spatial contrast in street and *place*, and in another literally but importantly superficial way. The great hillside square, falling steeply at one end towards the looping river, is lined with splendidly robust commercial

Richmond, Yorks: plan.

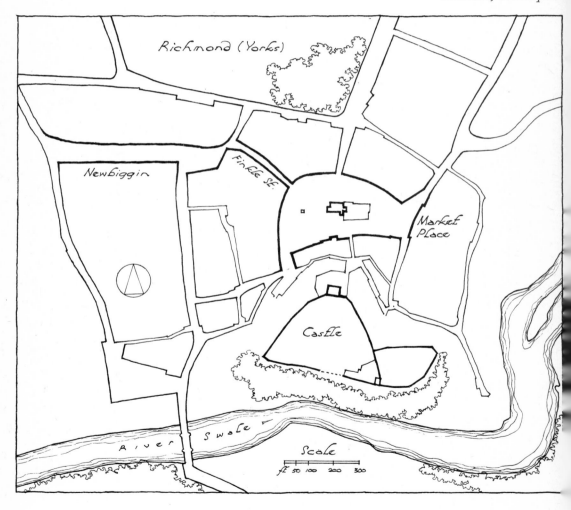

Richmond. A large curved market-place fronted by robust country-town buildings, with a church and a group of shops islanded in the middle, and backed by a great castle keep.

buildings. It also has an unusual combination of church and shops islanded in its middle, and is dominated by the great keep of the Norman castle rising gigantically over its roofs on one side. Five streets enter the square deviously and narrowly, one of them leaping up precipitously from the river bridge, and another, Finkle Street, narrow, lined with shops, nearly but not quite straight, connecting it by a dogleg with the contrasting domestic Newbiggin, wide, elongated, ordered though not formal, and diversified with trees. But besides all this, Richmond is remarkable also in that it has not fallen into the error of most of its kind in dealing with its road surfaces: and it deserves a special note of honour for the way it has kept its stone paving in Market Place and Newbiggin free from tar, though not, unfortunately from car.

93

Richmond. Looking out through a gateway's arch. A framed view from a town on to hilly country can afford a special pleasure.

Alnwick, Northumberland. The entrance to the town. Plain ashlar-fronted houses, castle barbican beyond, trees, cobbles – and cars.

And so one could go on through several hundred other country towns. These that we have looked at by way of example are no doubt rather special in their concentration of good architecture and fine townscape. Perhaps to come nearer the average we might have looked at Alnwick, Berwick,

Berwick, Northumberland. The main street through an arched opening in the town walls. The Town Hall stands forward from the street frontage to punctuate the view, and the roadway swings round it.

*Tewkesbury, Glos.
Unity and rhythm in
variety.*

Appleby, Barnard Castle, Thirsk, Kendal, Kirkby Lonsdale,
Boston, Oakham, Ludlow, Pershore, Tewkesbury, Malmes-
bury, Marlborough, Shaftesbury, Totnes, and so on down
the counties of England. They would have afforded us
examples enough. But selection from the general in the end
is invidious; so we can let the description of these three stand
for what is one of the glories of England, the townscape and
architecture of her country towns.

*Totnes, Devon. Rhythm
maintained up a rising
street, and a church tower
crowning the view on one
side.*

And, of course, her ten thousand villages. Townscape may not, perhaps, be the precise word to apply there, but the visual rewards are of the same kind: the unfolding scenes; the interplay of forms; the juxtaposition of foils; the delayed climax; the external feature that enriches the internal character; the way its roads, curving into and out of the central parts, give the village the character and identity of a

Dorchester, Oxon. The winding of the road through the village gives a comfortable sense of containment as well as changing views.

particular place, constitute it as a local climax and not merely an incident on the roadside. Because it would lead us into wild disproportion to attempt to analyse and exemplify these village characteristics and effects here[1], the mere mention of one or two examples must suffice – *Dorchester* in Oxfordshire, a village whose plan, as so often, is wholly determined by the road which wriggles through it, but where subtlety and

[1] See *The Anatomy of the Village* (Penguin Books, 1946).

97

Town and townscape

interest are added by the recessions and advances that occur in the lines of its buildings: *Blanchland* in Northumberland, where, in a secluded valley after a drive over wild moors, you dog-leg at an archway or over a bridge into the oasis of a square of cottages lying against the tower of the remains of an abbey that is now the village church: *Thaxted* in Essex, where the streets twist and turn to an irregular-shaped *place* with a great church riding above it.

Blanchland, Northumberland. An oasis among moors. Though its history is unrecorded, its plan-form and the continuity of its frontages and roof-lines indicate that the 'square' was planned as a whole. The staggered entrances contain the views in and out.

99

Thaxted, Essex. The twisting, closing-in and opening-out of the streets and the siting of the great church provide complicated and dramatic townscapes.

INDUSTRIAL TOWN

Then there are the industrial towns.

Of course most of what are now thought of as purely industrial towns were country towns before the Industrial Revolution engulfed them and changed their character – and come to that, strange as it may seem now, some places of notable beauty, like Chipping Campden, have seen the reverse of that process, being in their distant foundation industrial towns even though they have long ago lost that character.

Wigan, that town which through music-hall jokes has become established in popular mythology as the industrial town *par excellence*, was one of these country towns that were engulfed and transformed; and, as a consequence, though its general character and its architecture are far from being of the highest order, the townscape of its main streets is full of kinetic interest and liveliness.

100

Swindon is a more representative example of the towns that sprang up more or less new in the Industrial Revolution. In fact it only came into being in the form it has now because the Oxford dons of the time, more sensitive and active than the later ones who are also surrounded by a revolution in the means of transportation, successfully resisted a proposal to site a great railway works in the shadow of their dreaming spires. If, in saving Oxford, the new town that resulted twenty-five miles away did not acquire a distinguished character of its own, that is not altogether surprising: but still, no doubt because its new main streets followed the lines of old country lanes, it did develop some of the effects of kinetic townscape that save it from the standardized dullness it would otherwise have had.

And so we could go on through most of the industrial towns of Britain. Gaunt, mean, depressing, raw still, after a hundred years, as many of them are, they are nearly all redeemed a little, here and there, by features with some kinetic quality that require only a way of looking for their conscious appreciation.

Swindon, Wilts. A nineteenth-century street terminating on an older building.

VI HAPPY ACCIDENTS?

Towns are not static. Mostly they grow and intensify: sometimes they decline. Townscapes are not fixed and unchanging. A single new building, as we have seen, may drastically alter a whole range of visual effects, may produce good or bad new ones, may reduce or heighten old ones. The mere removal of a building or a series of buildings may do the same. What principles can be deduced for preserving and extending good townscape in our present towns, and for achieving it in new places?

It may perhaps be said that most of the effects we have observed in the towns that we have looked at are the result of happy accident. And so, no doubt, some of them may be – though that should not make such lessons as they may hold any the less valid for conscious undertakings in the future. But is that usual generalization always valid? A glance back at Oxford suggests that it is not. The unusual design of the Queen's College entrance buildings there may be remembered. At the critical central point on the unfolding concave side of High Street, among the solid-walled frontages of colleges and shops, the arrangement is of two pedimented end-pavilions connected by a curtain-wall with a tall open-sided cupola over a central gateway – a most complicated and sophisticated architectural arrangement. Considering this unusual form, it is difficult to believe that Hawksmoor conceived his building in isolation, that he did not deliberately give it this special design for a special effect in relation to this particular point in this particular street. Similarly it is almost as difficult to believe that Dean Aldrich was not aware of Turl Street as well as High Street when he designedly sited his tower of All Saints Church in the middle of the Turl

Oxford. Turl Street entering High Street. All Saints Church (the wallace on the right) steps forward right into the line of the street, which has to make a severe dog-leg round it. The flèche of a college chapel punctuates the inner view. A happy accident or an effect cunningly planned?

Street view. And to consider a natural form, as well as these architectural ones, there is that feature close by Queen's which contributes as much to High Street townscape as any of its buildings, including Queen's itself – the Sycamore of sycamores that bosoms out from All Souls. If ever there was a 'happy accident' one might think this was it. Yet that tree is certainly not more than 120 years old – and engravings of 150 years ago show a tree of about the same size in the same position. The earlier tree may perhaps have been a 'happy accident': but *this* later one certainly is not: it is the result of a conscious action designed to create a particular effect.

The same conscious choice of a rewarding site, and the deliberate designing of a building to make a telling use of it, must have operated widely in producing many of the effects that are now regarded as happy accidents. It was not that, in their early definition, the street lines which gave the opportunities for architectural effects were deliberately created with those effects in mind – nor indeed were they 'accidentally' created either: they were purposefully created, or at least they purposefully resulted out of various needs and intentions, for other functions. But if they were not in any way created with architectural possibilities in view, the opportunities they 'accidentally' afforded for those must often have been the reason why particular sites were chosen for special buildings and particular designs developed for them. Thus many a guildhall, many a market-house or other important building or feature occupying some telling position on a curve or a twist in a medieval street, or a key position in an open *place*, must almost certainly have been sited and designed deliberately to exploit an opportunity that was accidentally afforded – as indeed many an eighteenth-century town-hall (such as that at Berwick), or the University building at Bristol which has already been cited, illustrate for more recent times.

But whether or not these townscape effects came into being accidentally, their mere existence shows the value of the contribution they make to the continuing interest of our towns. And their characteristics show too that such effects can be created consciously and deliberately in new undertakings if we want them. Great architecture in noble buildings may not often occur. Even better-than-moderate architecture is not all that common. The average town consists of average architecture: and the average has been pretty low for the last century and more. But if we cannot achieve good architecture except in a few places, we can enjoy the pleasures and interests of townscape where it exists, and sometimes even newly create it in places where it is now absent.

TOWN AND TRAFFIC

10'-9"
HEADROOM

VII CAR AND CHARACTER

These qualities and attributes of townscape and town character that we have been looking at can be properly appreciated only in slow movement about a town and through unimpeded views of the different parts of it. The view from a closed car, for instance, if it is not of the car in front or at the side, is mostly too low for near buildings. The speed at which a car moves, except in a stop-go traffic jam when the mood is not one for architectural appreciation, is too great for the observation of all but the most general effects. And, anyhow, the attention of the driver, at least, should be on his driving rather than on the sights of the town. So the townscape pleasures of the street can only be got in any true and full measure by walking there.

It is becoming increasingly difficult to do so. Railed-off kerbs restrict movement. One-way streets become speed tracks. Main traffic is diverted into hitherto quiet streets. Noise afflicts the ears; exhaust-fumes rasp the throat and nostrils; the turmoil of moving cellulose jitters the nerves, blocks the view and threatens mutilation and sudden death. Even when the masses of motorized tin stand unused, their multi-coloured litter still deals death and destruction – if only to the view. Even when they are not themselves in evidence, the provisions for their use and control still obtrusively mar the urban scene – the trivial intrusions that accumulate to outrage; traffic signs; parking meters; giant directional and instructional lettering painted on road surfaces; double yellow lines, single yellow lines, dotted yellow lines paralleling kerbs; white lines dividing carriageways; car-spaced lines patterning parking sites. And, with these, there are the larger works; the destruction of colour and texture in the surfaces of

Beverley, Yorks. A new kind of wine in an old bottle-neck.

road spaces, where setts, cobbles and gravelled areas are
smoothed and smothered under a skin of the ubiquitous tar
that reduces everything to a neutral aridity – or, contrastingly,
the squalor and space-leakage of the pot-holed stone-strewn
surfaces in the rear-exposing sites of demolished buildings
that are left open to accommodate ever more vehicles left
uselessly standing about – these, too, are the consequences
of the car.

Even so the visual effects of this present ruin by motor are
felt less strongly by most people than is the mutual stultifica-
tion which the vehicles themselves produce. The more people
travel by car in the centre of a town the slower and less com-
fortably they travel. Motor vehicles crowd the streets to such
an extent that frequently, and especially at peak hours, they
can hardly move at all. And when they do arrive at where
they want to be, as often as not it requires a near-hopeless
search to find somewhere to leave them; and as often as not,
again, when the place is found, it is road space that is occupied
at the cost of frustrating other traffic. Private cars so crowd
the streets that they impede public transport. The slower and
more irregularly buses travel, the more people take to their
private cars in despair; and then the buses travel slower still.
It is a maddening vicious circle, a crazy nightmare of mutual
frustration. The centre of London has become a kind of hell
for most hours of the day. The large provincial cities are
nearly as bad. The moderate-sized places suffer in varying
degrees of intensity; but they all suffer. Even the little country
towns and villages, if they are on a main traffic route, or if
they have the misfortune to be attractive, suffer in the same
way.

Both as places to look at and as places merely to be in,
the centres of most towns are being murdered by motor.

And it will get worse, far worse. In ten years' time there
will be twice as many motor vehicles as there are now; in
thirty years three times as many; in fifty years there may be
four or five times as many.

Clearly the towns that we have now cannot accommodate
such traffic. Many will not be able to take even the increase
forecast for ten years' time, never mind that at the end of
the century. We are faced with the alternatives of largely

rebuilding our towns or restraining the traffic that is killing them.

Even if we could contemplate wholesale rebuilding, it is a physical and financial impossibility. The imperative pace cannot possibly be achieved. There is not a fraction of the labour force, not a fraction of the money, to do it in time.

We can, of course, do *some* of the work in *some* of the places – and produce the kind of devastation, the dismemberment, that the vastly superior resources of America have facilitated in their far inferior cities. In doing so we will make confusion as much worse confounded as has happened there: cities torn apart for super-highways, half-demolished for parking places, only to make traffic pour in in still greater volumes. We can make a local improvement here, and do a local rebuilding there, so as to ease traffic congestion at particular points – and almost always make it worse somewhere near by. For, the fact is, the more traffic in towns is given the opportunity to increase, the more it does so. Short of large-scale rebuilding, we can never now provide sufficient space in our towns for the natural uncontrolled increase of

Confusion worse confounded – as seen by Osbert Lancaster.
Daily Express, 2. iv. 64

"Nothing wrong at all, thank you, officer—it's just that I'm a terribly slow reader."

traffic that the next few decades will bring (as we can never except by rebuilding achieve the general segregation of vehicles from pedestrians by means of elevated 'walkways' at first-floor level or the ruin-spreading monorail systems which are so much advocated by many architects and planners). And we can by no means be certain that we could provide sufficient space even by rebuilding – if any semblance of the town as we have known it through history is to survive.

What it comes to is this. We have neither the means nor the time to rebuild our towns so as to make them capable of accommodating the total traffic that the near future will bring (which in any case is fortunate in view both of the architectural character and the historical interest of many of them, and of the uncertain quality of present-day architecture). In undertaking mere occasional improvements, we must inevitably, because of the scale and freedom that modern traffic movement requires, do destructive damage without producing any commensurate benefits, often indeed any long-term benefits at all. There is a danger amounting almost to certainty that if we continue in the way we are going we will bring about the ruin of our towns, without, in the end, achieving any solution at all of their traffic problems.

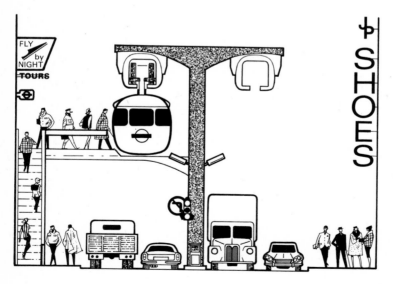

Murder most foul, or how to kill townscape. A serious proposal.

VIII LOOKING AND LIVING

Must we then despair of regaining for our towns the conditions of quietness, calm, spaciousness, freedom and safety
of movement which will permit the observing of their townscapes, the savouring of their characters, the enjoyment of the
opportunities they offer for social intercourse, and the pur-
suance, in general, of the benefits of town-living in ease and
comfort? And must we, if we cannot do that, despair of
making them adequate to the needs of modern traffic and the
traffic of the future?

The answer to both those questions is that we must truly
despair, and must stop the hopeless attempt, if by 'traffic' we
simply mean *all* the traffic of the town, all the unselected
traffic that all the demanding drivers may wish to pour into
it. The day has gone when town-planners could reasonably
be asked to 'plan the town to meet the needs of the traffic'.
There will have to be a different conception of the need now.
There can be no peaceful co-existence between the town and
the unrestricted motor. They are utterly incompatible. Unrestricted traffic will mean the death of the town. If we are
to continue to live in towns (and how can we help it?), the
conception for the future will have to be the reversal of what
it has been in the past; it will have to be that we must *plan
and regulate the traffic to meet the needs of the town.*

One way of attempting this has been suggested in the idea
of a road-using or 'congestion' tax. People are to pay for
using the roads – to pay variably according to the town, the
district and the street where they drive; according to the time
of day, the length of time when they drive, and the size of
vehicle. It sounds an incredibly complicated operation. But
in this age of remarkable technical devices it can be done.

113

And it is suggested that when people have to pay for using the roads they will use them less. Yet it is all hopeless. Unless the charges are penal in the extreme, people will still use their cars (as they still smoke cigarettes in spite of penal taxation and other discouragements). And if the charges are penal it will be socially unjust in that those who have the means will be able to buy what, if it is a right, should be a right reasonably available to all; and those with surplus money and no real need will be favoured against those whose need is essential though they have less money to satisfy it with – all of which is contrary to what is acceptable to modern society. To be acceptable, any system of variable restriction must be based on the degree of need rather than the degree of wealth.

Systems of that kind will be neither acceptable nor successful even in merely reducing traffic congestion. But it is not merely congestion we have to get rid of. We have to seek not merely relief from the worst of the hell made by modern traffic but actual release from it. The aim must be to exclude from town-centres all traffic except that which has an undeniable need to be there.

The principle should be this – *the only private traffic permitted within a town-centre should be traffic associated with the permanent occupancy and the functioning of the buildings and the utilities within it*. This means that among private vehicles only the cars of people living in the locality or the vehicles of persons or agencies servicing its buildings and their occupants should have entry into it. There should be no private cars or other private vehicles on its streets merely for the purpose of visiting the area or passing through it: and there should be no parking of cars in any public place within it. Persons visiting the locality to work, to shop, to transact business or merely to find some pleasure of one kind or another should use some form of public vehicle (or walk) to get about it.

Of course an essential rider to the imposition of restrictions on the use of private vehicles must be an enormous improvement in the availability of public ones. It is a sad thing that public transport in our larger cities, especially in London (where it used perhaps to be unequalled anywhere in the world), has been progressively declining as other traffic has increased. It has largely been a result of that increase and the

Banbury, Oxon. The market-place as car-park

114

congestion caused by it. When the reliability of public transport has been impaired because of traffic congestion, the vicious circle of reaction that has already been referred to sets in. In contrast to that, the results and demands of excessive private traffic in North American cities show what happens when there is little or no provision of public transport: and, while in ours it declines, those cities are now desperately attempting to overcome their increasing congestion by private vehicles through the belated establishment of the only alternative.

For public transport *is* the only alternative to strangulation by private transport. When comparison is made between the bus and the private car in relation to their passenger-carrying capacity in terms of road-space occupancy, the case for public transport is overwhelming. A high proportion of the private cars in towns carry only one person. A double-decker bus occupying little more than three times a car's road-space can carry sixty. Of course not all passenger movement can be undertaken by bus. In the absence of private cars, the halt, the infirm, the hurrying and various others will have to be provided for in an increase of taxis plying for hire. But not only will these forms of public-transport vehicles occupy in movement only a small fraction of the road-space taken up by private cars and be merely a small fraction of their numbers, they will also require little or none of the great areas occupied by empty cars littering the streets or standing about in parking places.

There will initially, without a doubt, be strong resistance by motorists to any restriction which seeks to exclude them from particular places. From the beginning they have had the freedom of all public highways. Yet *some* restraints on that freedom they have already had to accept – payment at parking meters, one-way street systems, exclusion of heavy vehicles from town streets where by-passes have been provided, traffic regulation generally. And indeed the disciplines of circumstance, especially the near-hopelessness of finding parking places, have already forced many to the acceptance of some self-imposed limitation on their use of their cars. But whether motorists like it or not, severe external limitation is now inevitable.

How can the limitation be operated so as to be both successful and equitable? The means is surely a very simple one. As vehicles have now to be licensed for use on any highway, so they can be required to be specially licensed for use on specified highways, particularly on central-town highways. Only specially licensed vehicles should penetrate into the central parts of a town beyond certain specified points. At these points there should be easily distinguishable signs forbidding entry to all vehicles except those displaying a licence or emblem permitting them to do so. The driver of any vehicle entering the limited area or precinct without a special licence will simply be subject to prosecution – with the usual consequences. The entry licences will be issued by the local licensing authority before whom a special case will need to be made in every individual application: and they will be available only to those living in the precinct or servicing buildings or utilities there.

*Exeter. A pedestrian
shopping street.*

In the operation of such a system, there will necessarily
be various refinements that cannot be gone into here. And
for its success a number of conditions will need to be met.
There will need to be reasonably direct ways round a precinct
to enable cross-town traffic to avoid it – something of a pre-
cinctal ring-road or by-pass. There will need to be sufficient
provision for the parking of cars near to lines of public
transport in the districts adjacent to the points of entry. And
in large cities there will have to be a number of central precincts instead of one very large one. But providing these and
similar needs are satisfied there is no reason at all why such
a system should not operate with simple smoothness and
success – and with no real hardship to anyone but rather with
general benefit to all.

IX A WAY OF REDEMPTION

An idea and the possibility of its application may be demonstrated better in a particular example than through a general statement of intention. And because that might be devised to make the possibility seem easier than in fact it may be, the use of a particular town as an example may be more profitable than demonstration through a theoretical one.

Since for various reasons it may be better not to identify it specifically, we may call our town Oldborough. It is situated on either side of a smallish river; is a regional centre at a crossing of trunk roads, a town of about 100,000 inhabitants, with a central area of great character contained within old city walls, a university partly inside and partly adjacent to the central area, and considerable twentieth-century industrial suburbs round about.

An external by-pass system was completed some years ago. It has diverted most of the through-traffic outside the town, especially the heavy industrial traffic. That has been a benefit; but it has reduced the traffic in the town centre by only some 15 per cent. After all, most of a town's traffic (except in a few special instances) is self-generated; and since the density of traffic has increased everywhere in the five years since the by-passes were completed, there is still as much congestion in Oldborough's medievally aligned streets as ever there was. The by-passes have alleviated the developing condition, but have not effected any cure. So a middle-ring system of relief-roads, running through the suburbs a mile or so beyond the town centre, is now planned. That too will be helpful. It will enable a lot of cross-town traffic to avoid the central area altogether. But it will not be enough. It will take years to complete; and even when it is finished and in use there will

Oldborough: an imaginary example showing how all vehicles except those associated with the people living in a precinct and those servicing the buildings there can be excluded from it. At all the entering places (marked solid black) there would be signs declaring 'No Entry' to all but vehicles holding a special licence to enter.

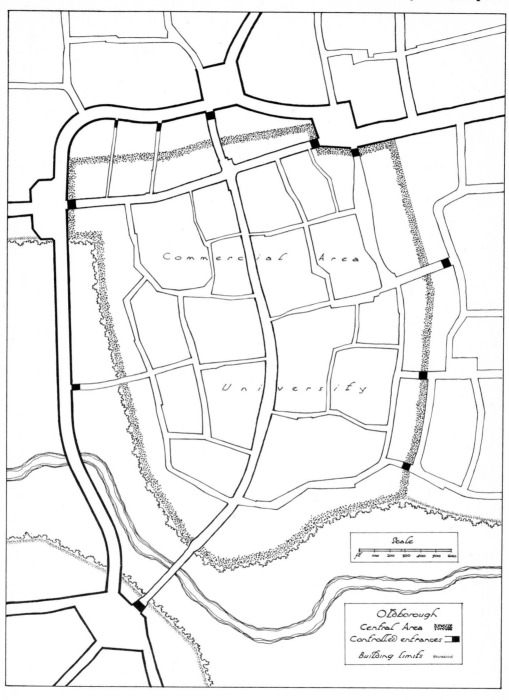

Commercial Area

University

Scale

FE 100 200 300 400 500 600

Oldborough
Central Area
Controlled entrances
Building limits

still be as much traffic clogging the central streets as there is
now, for cross-town traffic is only about 30 per cent of the
total traffic in the central area, and the relief afforded by
distantly providing for that traffic will soon be overtaken by
natural increase.

Something more must be done. New roads must be provided adjacent to the central area itself. But if they are to be
successful in bringing release to that area they must be more
than merely relief-roads. Relief-roads, while the old streets
remain open and readily accessible, will only partly reduce
congestion there; and in so far as road space is to some extent
freed it will be claimed for parking. So real release will be
as far off as ever. The new roads must not merely be relief-
roads. They must be *substitute-roads*; roads in substitution of
the old streets, to take off them all but the traffic that is
directly serving the buildings there. Further, if only directly
associated vehicles are to be allowed on those streets, these
substitute-roads must be sufficiently close in to the central
area for people to get there easily – which means that they
must not be more than the easy walking-distance of a few
hundred yards from the very central points.

At Oldborough there is an eminently satisfactory route for
a substitute-road. Part of it lies over flood-land which has
remained unbuilt on, part through an extensive slum district
which in any case needs immediate redevelopment; and only
a very short length involves any demolition of substantial
property. Once this road were built there would be no need
for any traffic at all, other than its own, to enter the central
area. It could not, however, be left at that, for unless there
were prohibition against entry, people would still drive and
park their cars there. So since persuasion by provision would
not be enough, enforced exclusion must be operated. And
it could be operated without any serious impediment or
hardship to anyone. There are four major points of entry to
the central area, and six minor ones. All that would need to
be done, with the substitute-roads available, would be to
indicate by signs at these points that there is No Entry
beyond them, except to specially licensed vehicles – and the
only specially licensed vehicles, as has already been said,
would be those belonging to the comparatively few residents

in the area, the vehicles servicing the buildings there, and such public-transport vehicles as may be deemed necessary. These public-transport vehicles would here be mainly taxis; though, if it were desirable, there could be a shuttle bus-service running from one end of the High Street to the other.

Of course there would need to be provisions ancillary to the new roads, notably places where cars which are prohibited from using the central streets could be conveniently left. There would need to be a sufficiency of parking-buildings conveniently placed in relation to the middle-ring road as well as others in relation to the substitute-roads. But most of these will be required in any case, so their necessity should not be charged against this creation of an almost traffic-free precinct.

Almost traffic-free, but not quite. There would still, if this plan were adopted, be a trickle of traffic about these central Oldborough streets: sufficient to maintain some little liveliness there, but far from so much as to cause danger or distraction. And that is as it should be. Even small-scale pedestrian precincts, such as those that are now being made in some towns, are apt to appear dead and dull, lacking in liveliness, for most of the time outside the busiest shopping hours. The whole central area of a town (this at Oldborough being half a mile long by a third of a mile wide) would suffer seriously in attractiveness if there were no vehicle movement at all about it – even Venice has its traffic in movement along scores of little canals as well as the grand ones. We must not kill our towns by excessive control. But in any case the total exclusion and prohibition of motor vehicles from its centre is impossible if a town is to live. Goods and articles of all kinds must be moved about in it. The need is to control severely but not to abolish: to control so that only the traffic essential to the life of an area which otherwise would be congested can enter and move about it. So by these means these central streets of Oldborough could be made safe and pleasant again. There would be no parked cars anywhere on the streets of the precinct. There would be just the trickle of wheeled traffic that would provide incident and movement to contribute to their liveliness. People going about there, loitering or hurrying, could do so on widened pavements adjacent to lightly used roadways. And besides attending to their business and their social pleasures they could again observe the visual riches that Oldborough's townscape provides – they could do this, that is to say, if only (and only if) they and their government agencies take the clear and necessary decisions to make it possible.

If this could be done for Oldborough it could equally be done for other towns. It may be that the configuration of Oldborough's form and street-plan lends itself more readily to adaptation for the constitution of a precinct than do most. In some towns the opportunity may be even more readily available, may even in the main exist now. Others may not present the opportunity so obviously. But something of this kind could be done almost everywhere. And by doing it we could redeem town and townscape from this particular enemy of traffic that now threatens to destroy them.

122

York: a street for only occasional local vehicles.

TOWN AND TOWER

X FASHION PARADE

The other enemy that threatens and has indeed already achieved serious and permanent damage to townscape and town character is the new fashion for high buildings.

Hitherto, over all the hundreds of years of history, roof-lines have been of much the same level throughout the extent of each town, increasing a little towards the centre as it has grown larger. Now, suddenly and astonishingly, within the last few years a dramatic change has come about. In the larger cities great towers and slabs of buildings have begun to appear, riding high over the general roof-level and dwarfing even the spires and church towers which have until recently held dominion in the lower sky. They are beginning to appear in the smaller towns and cities also. And even in the quiet little country towns that are hardly bigger than a village. Villages themselves have their projected tower-buildings. There are even towers in the fields. Towers have become the latest building fashion.

Fashion, the latest mode, is a term which accurately describes them. They are a new thing, a novelty (though quite old hat in the New World). And since architecture is today of all professional activities the most subject to fashion, the ambition of almost every architect is to build a tower wherever he can get the opportunity to do so. New materials, new techniques of building, have made it easier than before to build high. It is therefore proper and desirable to build high – so the argument runs, if argument it can be called. And so the new fashion for high buildings, for doing something merely because it can be done, and because in doing it the designers and their clients get a glow of personal satisfaction regardless of wider considerations – so the fashion

Aylesbury, Bucks. Big Brother in a country town. An extension to County Council offices. Described by an admirer as 'good enough to join the select company of big buildings that command affection'. Command, certainly. But affection?

125

for towers and slabs, and particularly for towers, has begun to hump and lump about our urban skylines almost before the majority of people have realized it, and certainly before its full implications have been considered.

One of the characteristics of fashion is that it may turn out to be only temporary. But the results of this particular fashion will be all too permanent. The fashion may change but the buildings will remain. A year or two of this kind of building can alter irretrievably the effects that have been created in our towns over the centuries – has already done so in many places. Never before has it been possible to effect so much change in so short a time, and by a single building.

Since we have been considering Oxford at some length, it is not inappropriate to take it, and Cambridge too, as initial examples of what has been happening, or what has been threatening to happen. At Cambridge in the last year or two, the University itself (which of all bodies one might have expected to have some regard for the character of its setting) has been proposing the erection of tower-buildings at the very heart and centre of that association of university, college and town buildings which constitute its boasted near-unique character as a university-town. It is necessary to redevelop the site of the old New-Museums science buildings near-by the market-place. At first the University proposed, and pressed the town-planning authority to permit, three tower-buildings, two rising to over 200 feet and one to 150 feet (the present highest buildings in the town, excluding church towers and such-like, being 50–60 feet). When the planning authority refused to countenance this, pointing out the devastating effect that these towers would have on notable scenes in the town, the view of King's College from the Backs, the views of various colleges and a great many street views, the University's distinguished architect, protesting strongly and insisting that he must have towers of some sort or he would resign, reduced them to 110 feet and 90 feet. When the planning authority refused to permit towers of even that height, the University, at the Public Inquiry that was held into the design, pleaded that it was essential to scientific learning that they should have such towers. The expert Inspector who held the Inquiry said that that was

Cambridge. Tower-buildings proposed by the University seen beyond King's College from the Backs. (The drawings superimposed on the photograph are intended to show only the height an bulk of the towers, not any actually proposed architectural treatment of them. Likewise on the picture below.)

Cambridge. The effect the proposed towers would have on a town street.

neither true nor desirable, and that towers should not be allowed. The Minister concerned with town-planning, no doubt advised by some anonymous administrative civil servant who had fallen for the fashion, overruled his own professional expert and said that the towers would do no harm and should be built. So did the Royal Fine Art Commission. So that was evidently to be that: and the historical character of Cambridge was to be blown sky-high with towers. Then the towery architect, having forced the matter so far, retired for reasons that had nothing to do with this particular project, and the new architect who was appointed didn't think towers were at all necessary, and abandoned them. So the whole character of Cambridge, after its slow evolution over 600 years, had been put at the whim of a single determined architect, and has only been saved because he decided to transfer his activities elsewhere. That is the extremity to which the fashion of tower-building has brought even our most distinguished towns.

At Oxford the risk was higher but the escape less narrow. There (by the University again) the proposal was for a single tower of some twenty-five storeys rising 260 feet into the sky, the general level of building in the city, at 30–40 feet, being even lower than at Cambridge. It was to be a town-dominating tower designed for no less distinguished a purpose than housing animals used in zoological experiment and research: a sort of aerial rabbit warren. Fortunately, this megalomaniac project was defeated within the University itself – though only after formidable lobbying and controversy – and the deplorable spectacle of the University publicly fighting to ruin its city was avoided. So Oxford too has been temporarily saved from the worst[1] of the fashionable fate that has overtaken other towns. But that proposals like these should have been made in towns like these (and by people who are thought to be enlightened) shows how strong an appeal the new fashion is making even in the most unexpected quarters.

Not that academic enlightenment seems generally to extend

---

[1] Worst, because the University has nevertheless gone some regrettable length (and height) in the fat sub-tower of its new engineering and nuclear physics buildings at the top of the second finest street in the city, St Giles.

to the environment outside the academic precinct. At Durham, some years ago, at a Public Inquiry, the University joined with the planning authority, the shop-keepers and the trades unions, in actually welcoming the proposed construction of a giant power-station complex which, as a close neighbour, would have reduced the Cathedral, the University buildings themselves, and the whole centre of that small city, to trivial insignificance; and it was left to two or three private citizens, in an apparently forlorn hope, to defeat the monstrous intention.

But if Oxford and Cambridge (and Durham) have so far been saved from affliction by towers, half the large towns in the country, and some of the smaller ones as well, have already, in a mere matter of a year or two, been irretrievably changed. London has sprouted towers at fortuitous intervals all over the place. Manchester, Birmingham, Newcastle, and other cities of their kind have inflicted great weals on their skylines in an orgy of self-flagellation. Coventry, having just completed a new cathedral, has immediately over-topped it, next door, by the soaring tower of a student hostel. Many other medium-sized towns have suffered themselves to be topped by towers. And safety has not lain in smallness, as

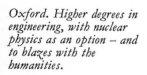

Oxford. Higher degrees in engineering, with nuclear physics as an option – and to blazes with the humanities.

Henley's projected (and Ministerially approved) fifteen-storey hill-crowning flats have only too amply proved. The fashion for towers has swept the country like a contagious disease.

Of course, a new fashion need not necessarily be a bad one. It may indeed be a very good one. Old towns, as well as new, must accept new ways of building and new kinds of building. New forms should not be ruled out merely because they are unfamiliar. But neither should they be accepted merely because they are novel. And because this particular fashion can have such permanent results, it is especially necessary to consider how far the conditions which have created it are sound, how far the acceptance of those conditions is desirable in its effect on the design of individual buildings, and whether or not this effect is acceptable in the total creation, the town, which the individual buildings collectively make. It is astonishing to think that these matters have never yet been given any serious authoritative consideration. It may be that they have been ignored because they may seem humdrum and sober against the intoxication of building monuments. But dull and restrictive though they are they are infinitely more important than the excitements of architectural megalomania.

XI WHY HIGH?

To begin with, there is the argument that we should build high because it has become easier to do so. This in itself is clearly fallacious if it ignores the effects of the buildings which result. It could, nevertheless, be held to be strongly in their favour if economic and similar arguments could be produced in support of high buildings – if it could be shown, for example, that the new materials and new techniques which make building high more readily possible also make it so much cheaper that it is essential in the general interest that we should build that way.

But that is not so. Comparative costs of commercial buildings in high towers and in horizontal structures are hard to come by; but comparative costs for the building of flats are available. It is known, for example, that the construction costs per square foot of floor-space are about 40 per cent more for eight-storey buildings than for three-storey buildings; and about 50 per cent more for twelve-storey buildings. They are some 30 per cent and 40 per cent more, respectively, for eight-storey and twelve-storey buildings as against four-storey buildings where lifts are not installed. They are over 20 per cent more for eight-storeys and some 25 per cent more for twelve-storeys, as against the five storeys at which lifts become indispensable. Even the maintenance and service costs of an eight-storey building are 36 per cent more than those for a three- or four-storey building of the same floor area. And it has to be remembered that, though proportionate construction costs do not rise progressively with the height of a building, they do, nevertheless, rise steadily with each additional storey. So that, at the twenty-five and thirty storeys at which flats are now beginning to be built, the cost may perhaps be between two-thirds and three-quarters as high again, as against those of three- or four-storey buildings with the same accommodation in the more normal horizontal form.[1] If these are the figures for flats, those for offices and other uses in tower-buildings must not be entirely dissimilar, and it is clear from them that the high fashion is also an extremely expensive one – so expensive indeed that it must already have cost the country unnecessary scores of millions of pounds.

Another argument advanced in favour of building high is that it saves space. It is held that it keeps the town compact and so lessens urban encroachment on the countryside. This again is not so. It would no doubt be so if the only considera-tion were to get as much accommodation as possible on to every piece of land. But that would simply be urban anarchy. There are other considerations, even in relation to mere con-venience, let alone in relation to visual amenity – considera-tions of light, air, the right to some sky, the generation of traffic, the parking of vehicles, the effects of over-concentrat-ing people in one small area, the effects of shadow and wind, and so on and so on. To safeguard these considerations statutory town-planning schemes very properly impose con-trolling regulations on the occupancy of space. For houses and flats the control is generally imposed in terms of popula-tion – such and such a number of persons living on each acre. For other types of building it is generally in terms of site-occupancy in relation to floor-space – a 'plot ratio' which lays down that a site can accommodate a prescribed amount of floor-space in buildings in proportion to the size of its total ground area. Building in the centre of Cambridge, to take a not-untypical example, is limited by a plot ratio of $2\frac{1}{4}$ to 1; which means that a site can contain $2\frac{1}{4}$ times as much floor-space as it has ground area. This in turn means that (*a*) other regulations permitting, the whole of the site can be covered by a two-storey building rising to three storeys

---

[1] Figures based on tables in papers by: (1) P. A. Stone, 'Economics of Housing Urban Development', *Jnl of Royal Statistical Society* (Series A), vol. 122, pt. 4, 1958; and (2) Nathaniel Lichfield, *Jnl of Royal Institute of Chartered Surveyors*, Sept. 1960. And a recent (1966) report in *The Times* shows that in Birmingham the *economic* rent of a two-bedroom flat in a multi-storey building is £348 a year whereas the economic rent of a two-bedroom house is £262.

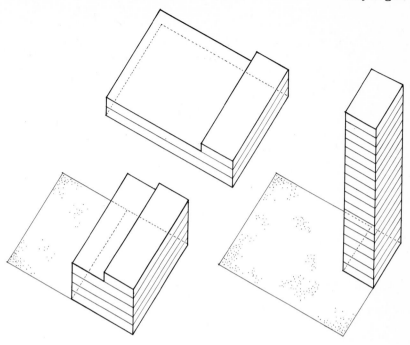

The effect of plot-ratios.

over a quarter of the area; or (*b*) a four-storey building can be erected over half the site, rising to five storeys over a quarter of the site area, the remaining half of the site being left open; and so on. In these proportions of site coverage an eighteen-storey building, for instance, could occupy (*c*) an eighth of the site. But at whatever height the building may be erected, the controlling formula of floor-space in proportion to site area remains. Regulations of this kind apply in all our towns.

It is much the same with the other method of controlling the occupancy of space – that relating to houses and flats. It is true that here very dense site occupancy may only be achieved by building high – the kind of occupancy which is achieved in the grossly overcrowded parts of central London where a density of up to 200 persons or rooms per acre is permitted. But no one concerned with reasonable conditions of living defends such densities except in the circumstances prevailing in such a situation – and many maintain that they are indefensible even there. Even for large cities the generally

133

accepted maximum density outside such exceptional circumstances is half that – at 100 rooms per acre. And that density in no way, in itself, brings very high buildings into being. It can be achieved indeed without any buildings rising to more than four storeys in height.[1] But even 100 rooms per acre is generally held to be too high except for the middle-ring quarters of very large cities: and, for most towns, the acceptable maximum housing density is generally about 70 rooms per acre. To achieve that, no building need of necessity be more than three storeys high: and if it *is* built higher, the maximum density remains, and no more accommodation or population can be got on to the ground because of its being so.

From this it is clear that the contention that building high lessens the town's physical encroachment on the countryside is untrue so far as mere area is concerned. It is also clear that it saves no ground space at all in terms of the town as a whole.

What it *can* do is to free a proportion of individual *site* space. That is what could happen in the examples given above, where it was said that on a site with a plot ratio of $2\frac{1}{4}$ to 1, the building might be one covering quarter of the site to nine storeys or one of eighteen storeys over one-eighth of the site, and so on. In this sense it is obvious that the higher the building, the greater may be the amount of free unbuilt-on space for use as gardens, car-parks and other purposes at its base.

This theoretical advantage is rarely, if ever, exploited by high buildings in town centres, for the obvious reason that it involves the loss of valuable building-frontage at street level. The almost invariable form of building in these instances is a one- or two-storey *podium* of shops and similar establishments covering the whole site, with a tower-building rising above part of this, the only 'freed' space being roof space which, in the English climate at any rate, is of very little use to anyone. For the general appearance of the town

[1] See *Flats and Houses,* 1958, published by HMSO for the Ministry of Housing and Local Government, where an example in design, at 100 persons or rooms per acre, shows 26 per cent of the rooms in two-storey buildings and 74 per cent in four-storey buildings.

Leicester. Pygmies and giants. Architects building monuments to themselves?

at ordinary level it may be as well that this is so, for a city of towers standing in windy detachment is unlikely to be either very attractive or very convenient. But whether that is so or not, the fact remains that this alleged advantage of building high is rarely, if ever, exploited in commercial quarters.

In residential quarters it is exploited more often. And there is some force, in relation to each individual site considered independently, that it should be so where high density development is undertaken. In the more normal maximum densities, however, outside the central and near-central areas of great cities – i.e., at densities of 70 persons per acre and less – it is highly questionable both from the public and from private interests whether common open grounds are more satisfactory than private gardens of even very small size. And, in any case, even where high buildings may to some degree be defensible for limited private reasons in that they free ground space within their own site, they do that at the expense of the sky to which near-by lower buildings also have a claim. So that in at least an equal degree they are, in that, against the public interest. Moreover they have hitherto frequently been sited adjoining public open spaces. Many of the tower blocks of flats in public housing in London, for example, have deliberately been sited on the boundaries of parks, heaths and commons, so that their inhabitants may enjoy the benefits of those areas both in the views from their windows and in the use of their ground. Indeed, the overcrowding of these developments has generally been tolerable only because of the immediate proximity of these open spaces. In this way they have been dependent on borrowed space – and in this they have not been defensible.

Besides using borrowed space and borrowed sky for their own strictly individual purposes, high buildings steal that space and that sky – a widely extended and not merely local sky – from the rest of the town. And, in stealing them, they are far more likely than not to injure them, and consequently the town as a whole, in the further sense in which it is now necessary to consider the matter, namely in the sense of amenity.

XII   WHY NOT

Architectural and amenity values are important in all towns
and cities. And besides their visual considerations so are their
social implications.[1]

Consider first the effect of a tower-building, or a group of
tower-buildings, on its immediate surroundings. The result
is bound to be disruptive. A tower-building is bound to affect
the scale of the buildings that are seen with it. If these buildings have been designed along with the high building to
make a composite and self-contained whole, the general *local*
effect may (depending of course on the quality of the design)
be impressive in itself. But this can rarely happen in the
central area of an existing town. There, almost invariably a
tower-building will be *imposed* on its setting. And the almost
invariable effect, when it is, will be that of overbearing ill-
neighbourliness, the self-assertive domination of one element
that bears no relation to and has no care for the rest of the
members of the community of buildings round about. It is
then a kind of architectural gangsterism.

The difference in effect, between the tower-building which
is designed as part of a rare composite whole and that which
is not, can be seen in two recent developments in the same
quarter of London. The Shell tower (whatever one may
think of its design in the narrowly limited architectural sense,
and whatever its effects on the wider parts of the city outside
its immediate setting) may perhaps be regarded as having
something at least in its favour, in the purely local sense, in

---

[1] Leaving aside, since they are outside our consideration here, the immense
social problems that *living* in high flats give rise to. And people's preferences too.
A survey in 1967 (reported in the *Sunday Times*) shows that only one in one hundred
of the people interviewed would wish to live in a tower-building if they had open
preference.

that it is but one element in a deliberately designed and large-scale composite whole. In contrast, the Vickers tower, farther upstream on the opposite embankment, though a far better building in itself, is essentially an anarchic building of the most aggressive type, lifting its great height up into the sky regardless of the Tate Gallery next door, the Houses of Parliament a few hundred yards away, and any of the near and far buildings, streets and other places from which it can be seen.

Another London tower-block, or set of tower-blocks, illustrates the effect that this kind of building is bound to have on any street to which it is applied. The Victoria Street which existed until recently may not have been a street of much architectural distinction. But it did have a certain character, a cohesion, a specific form – the character and cohesion of a contained canyon-like metropolitan street. Now, at the western end of its northern side, it has no cohesive character or specific form at all. There are the two-storey *podia* which tower-blocks are always given in English town-centres; and above them, sometimes at right angles to the street, and sometimes parallel to it, there rise high slabs and a great tower against a tattered skyline. The street has gone (and the old scale of distances associated with the street); and in its place there is something which bears little or no recognizable relation to the street line or to the buildings which are left along it.

London. Private towers outrival the Houses of Parliament.

These two tower-buildings serve also to illustrate other effects – effects which are felt far beyond their own locality. The Vickers building offers a warning example of how a tower-building can unexpectedly dominate scenes so far distant as to be thought quite beyond its influence. Its effect on Whitehall, as far as nearly a mile away, has already been mentioned. St James's Street is also a mile away in a different direction: and running down from Piccadilly to St James's Palace, with, until recently, only the trees of the park seen beyond, it is now wholly dominated by that distant tower (as well as by another more recent near-by building) rising straight into the sky beyond the Palace on its central axis – and not merely is it dominated visually, its once fine scale has been destroyed by that unwelcome and unwanted but now all too permanent guest.

That kind of thing happens, of course – and it happens
frequently and apparently unpredictably – simply because in
a natural-grown city the street-system makes no regular and
obvious patterns. On a simple grid-iron plan there are no
architectural termini to street vistas: each vista merely
wanders out into a hazy distance of sky above some far-away
vanishing point. The buildings wall the interminable straight
streets in, and most views of them are sidelong. So in, say,
New York (and it is absurd how frequently canyon-streeted
New York is quoted in defence of these very differently
spaced London towers)[1] – there, and in similar places, the
street-picture is nothing like so much at the mercy of unconsidered incidents, whether near or far, as are the street-
pictures in London, Oxford, Cambridge and most European

[1] And even the famous skyline of Lower Manhattan as seen from the waterfront
has now been spoiled by a single wrong building – an enormous flat *slab* rising
among the soaring towers.

cities and towns. Here on gently curving, rapidly twisting and totally jumbled street-patterns it is nearly impossible to tell in advance what the effect of a high building will be on the other parts of the town outside the building's own immediate locality. It is so difficult as to be nearly impossible to judge, until after the event, whether or not, in all the various and varying street alignments that constitute a town, a new high building will unexpectedly emerge over intervening roofs at some street's slight change of direction, at some opening-out of a street-picture, or because of an incidental declivity in a road or a casual gap in a roof-line. The far formal termination of a street, and its immediate reduction in scale by a distant object, such as the Vickers building has produced in London on Whitehall and St James's Street, or the Hilton building on Baker Street, may quite well happen precisely in kind in other towns: but, even if it does not, sufficient other possibilities of disruption can occur as to put anyone who cares for a town in a perpetual state of alarm and despondency – unless the possibility is in fact rendered impossible by some order or regulation (such as a deliberate limitation of height through various parts of a town) being made to prevent it.

The incidental and unexpected effects made by slim spires and church towers, or even by so considerable a structure as a dome, are, of course, among the main delights of townscape in a natural-grown town. But the effects created by lumpish tower-buildings are of an altogether different kind. It becomes, there, a matter of scale, a matter of volume. It becomes a matter of a resounding deafening shout, as against the slight almost tentative architectural statement of a spire or the rounded phrasing of a dome. And how far and how powerfully the different kind of statement by a tower-building will resound and echo over far parts of a town is, as has been said, unpredictable.

Although the architectural quality of a building may not be its most significant attribute in the observing of townscape in general, it is, of course, as has been said, of prime importance in its effect on the appreciation of character. A single bad building, even when it is of usual height, can go far to destroy the character of the parts of the street adjacent

London: Upper Regent Street. All Souls Church with the BBC extension beyond. An old townscape feature subdued.

London: St James's Park.
Rus in urbe, *1960*.

to it. But its effect is limited to those parts. It can quickly be out of sight and put out of mind. But a tower-building cannot. It rears up insistently. If its effect is bad even when it is a good building, it is worse when it is a bad one; and its crime of disruption is then made doubly criminal by its own so widely advertised badness.

142

St James's Park.
Town Park, 1962.

London: Kensington Gardens, 1968.

Kensington Gardens with the new Knightsbridge Barracks.

And it is not merely the effect on streets. The Victoria Street towers in London, for example, dominate other urban scenes as well. Over the roofs of intervening streets they intrude in a most powerful way into St James's Park and Green Park, and as a consequence they have seriously reduced the scale and apparent size of these open spaces. The new   143

Hilton tower at the hinge-point of the whole royal park
sequence has had an even more extensive effect. It was the
Shell tower, seen from the Serpentine Bridge, that first among
recent buildings somewhat usurped the sky in the view at the
end of the long Hyde Park lake, where hitherto no ordinary
buildings of the surrounding great city had been visible. It
did so even though it is *three* miles away. But now the Hilton
tower has stepped up, bigger and bolder and nearer at hand,
and has altogether out-savaged the earlier intruder. And
more recently the soaring tower of Knightsbridge Barracks
and other adjacent towers will have added to its disruptive
effect.

With these buildings rising into the sky, the great scale and
the whole character of the wonderful sequence of royal parks
as London's *rus in urbe* has been changed. Something of the
same kind has happened to that other royal demesne, Richmond Park, as well. There tower-blocks of flats now bring
the city into what, until a few years ago, was a great stretch
of semi-wild country without a sign of the vast wen which
surrounded it. But then the same thing has happened also to
many of the commons, the heaths and the public parks – the
high buildings of London have reduced their scale and
changed their character. It has happened incidentally and
accidentally, of course. No one has intended it. Even the
official planners never gave sufficient care to realize that it
would happen. But that makes it all the more sad – and all the
more an object lesson for others to avoid; an object lesson

144

to remind Cambridge, for example, of what its tower-buildings would do to that unique sequence of urban landscape, its Backs: but one which no doubt would be wasted on Oxford, whose University, hysterical with concern over a plan to put a surface-lying road across a dank meadow, has nevertheless without so much as a thought destroyed the character, the scale, the sense of remoteness of its own beautiful University Parks by putting high buildings against its borders.

More distant country spaces as well as internal urban spaces are affected in the same way. Where there are high buildings at the edge of a large town, or even at the centre of a smaller one, they proclaim the town from a distance, and in this sense heighten its visual encroachment on the countryside. It may be said that church spires and cathedral towers have done this for centuries. But there is a world of difference between a slim vanishing spire, probably, in England, seen beyond trees, or the long nave and towers of a cathedral riding over town roofs – there is a great difference between these and the high heavy chopped-off silhouette of today's tower-buildings. There is a world of difference between dreaming spires (whether at Oxford or Cambridge or anywhere else) and teeming towers (whether occupied by flat-dwellers, office workers, dons, students or rabbits). And the difference is not merely an architectural one. It is one of profound social significance as well.

Which brings us to a final consideration in all this. It is

145

some decades now since anyone spoke much of the need for the observance of a social hierarchy in buildings. Once that was held to be a matter of high importance in civic design. In the fashion for tower-building it has been ignored and treated with contempt. But it still, surely, must be a valid and proper concept unless our values have become wholly corrupted. There is surely something offensive to spiritual values that the Victoria Street tower-block complex of commercial offices should reduce to trivial insignificance the tall campanile of Westminster Cathedral which has hitherto occupied that part of the London sky. There is surely something offensive to social values that the headquarters of a single commercial company in the Vickers tower should subdue Westminster Abbey, the Houses of Parliament and the whole range of government buildings in Whitehall; and that another similar structure not far away (the Shell tower) should do the same to the metropolitan centre of government. There is surely something peculiarly offensive to human dignity that at Oxford it should be proposed that a tower occupied by rabbits, mice and earthworms, should dwarf every other building in a city which in the past has made some not inconsiderable contribution to the development of the human mind and spirit. There is surely something unacceptably uncivil that a single tower of private flats should ride high over a whole small town, as is proposed at Henley.

In sum, it is surely wrong that one or more individual private interest should subdue the skyline of any town against the interests of the rest of the community. It is, of course, an excellent thing that the skyline should be diversified. It might perhaps be argued that it is less outrageous that it should be diversified by towers occupied by people than by the lumps of public utilities in gas-works, electricity works and such-like, which have so often dominated a town in the past – were it not that the towers themselves are generally as big and even more dominating than those utilities. But the proper elements of diversification are surely still those associated with spiritual values, as in church spires and towers, or at least with the general community according to the manner that has operated since towns were first created.

Glasgow: University Library. A justified tower-building.

Town and tower

There are, of course, places where a new appropriately designed tower (but rarely a high slab) can still be made an acceptable, even a welcome, contribution to the skyline. But it can only be acceptable if it is associated with a special and appropriate purpose. That purpose must be a public one. It could be a purpose related to some governmental or cultural function. But even then it must have some symbolic significance and not be merely a structure occupied for the common everyday working or living purposes of even governmental or cultural activity. Thus, to give an example, a tower used as a university library (such as the tower of the new university library at Glasgow) might be appropriate and acceptable, whereas one merely providing living quarters for university students would not.[1]

What it comes to is simply this: that even if our spiritual values have so far declined that the argument relating to them is no longer valid, the final contention remains that no single private interest, no minority of private interests, should be permitted to dominate a town architecturally, any more than it should do so socially.

And here we can sum up the matter generally. Building in high towers or slabs serves no essential public or private purpose. It is more costly in mere money. It does not save land. If it sometimes frees ground space it does so at the expense of other buildings' sky-space. It does not keep the town compact. It does not preserve the countryside, but, on the contrary, obtrudes upon it. It is architecturally anarchic. It ruins the scale of surrounding buildings, indeed of a wide locality round about. It can produce unexpected and destructive effects on near and far street-pictures. It reduces the scale and injures the character of near-by open spaces. It is offensive in the hierarchy of the town, subduing spiritual cultural and civic buildings to insignificance. If it satisfies an architect's megalomania and his client's desire for prestige, these are not conditions which can be permitted to be

---

[1] Which is not to say that the groups of towers of living quarters at the new University of Essex, for instance, are unacceptable. That kind of arrangement is a wholly different matter since the buildings are situated in the countryside, not in a town, and are related to a single separated community. As such the basis for the judgement of their acceptability or otherwise lies in considerations of rural rather than civic appropriateness.

achieved at the expense of a town. It is a mere fashion: a fashion which should now be outlawed before, in its mad progress, it irretrievably ruins every remaining town in the kingdom.

But what of the towns that are already ruined? Mistakes in building in the past were not only more limited in their effects, they were generally less difficult of correction than these will be. Who, now, will pull these towers down? Is there any possible likelihood that when their builders' revels are over these cloud-capp'd towers shall dissolve

> And, like an insubstantial pageant faded,
> Leave not a rack behind?

Alas, there is not. These buildings which in a few years have so utterly changed so many of our towns, and which have done so not because after careful deliberation it was thought good that they should be changed in this way, but merely out of the uncontrolled arrogance and irresponsibility of a few people – these towers, alas, will not dissolve. They are all too many and too substantial. They cannot now, like the regardless attitude that brought them about, be corrected. They are here to stay. And it is a bitter consideration that the only way to lessen their effect, stuck up as they mostly are, in London at least, like monstrous Aunt Sallys, half a mile and more apart on the skyline, may be to build more where they are – to build more so as to form limited (though all too numerous) clusters of half a dozen or so where they could produce an interplay against each other which may at least show some compositional purpose and effect, instead of a single insane disregard of everything else in the city.

Yet at least the still unaffected places, the still undisrupted towns and villages, may be saved. And it may, even, not be too much to hope that architects may again learn some humility, so that, while the cost of redemption will have been monstrously great, at least *something* will have been gained from the disaster.

CONCLUSION

As was indicated at the beginning, we have been concerned here only with the physical form and appearance of towns, with their looks, their visual character; with the things, the influences, the requirements which affect and determine that appearance and character, and which condition the possibilities of observing them. And we have been concerned only with their central parts, their town-centres; and mainly with the best of them at that – with cathedral-cities, the old medium-sized towns, the market towns, the country towns. We have not been concerned with the manifold problems of general town-planning, nor with architecture in the narrower sense.

There are all manner of other problems in our towns that need attention. There are dark areas of slums that must be cleared and redeveloped. There are vast twilight areas of grim nineteenth-century streets that need rehabilitating, revitalizing, enlivening. There is need for new open spaces and playing fields, with new pathways connecting them, away from the turmoil of traffic, and, perhaps, in the smaller towns, leading out into the open country. There is need for new schools, new libraries, new social institutions of various kinds. In the localities outside the town-centre, as well as in the centre itself, the pressing problems of modern traffic demand attention – the provision of new radial and cross-town roads; freeways, congestion-free exchange-points, underground and multi-storey parking places; perhaps monorail and other transport systems; certainly the protection of living areas against extraneous traffic. There is need for a general (but not over-zealous) tidying up, for the planting of trees, for the careful design and siting of a host of necessary minor provisions like bus-shelters, telephone-boxes, lamp standards, direction signs and so on. There is an enormous amount to be done even to make the living and working quarters of towns function properly, let alone be better, more satisfying, pleasanter places to inhabit. It is not only the town-centres that need more care for their present condition, more thought for their future. The whole of every town needs it too.

Even in the town-centres themselves, and even in the limited consideration of their mere looks, there are many not-unimportant matters that have been referred to only in passing or not at all – the design of shop frontages, especially of their facias and their advertisement displays; the placing of trees; the paving of public surfaces; the design and siting of the multitude of small structures, signs, utility provisions of all kinds that are necessary in the modern town. And so on and so on. All that has been attempted here, besides indicating how townscape can best be appreciated and ob-served, is how the main attributes of character, in our older towns in particular, have been established; how that estab-lished character can be conserved and preserved if it is thought desirable that it should be; and what the main present dis-ruptions and threats to that character are.

The arguments against these disruptions, the ways of avoiding these threats, are clear and obvious. If architects and their clients could be persuaded to have a closer regard to what exists at present; if town-planning powers were exercised with more vigour and understanding; if the authorities concerned were to display more initiative and decision in undertaking works that must be undertaken and in enforcing disciplines that must be enforced; if the various methods of conserving the character of our towns while at the same time organizing them to function according to modern needs were adopted and pursued – if these things were done then conservation would be almost self-operating.

It is, in the end, merely a question of whether we want to do it, whether we put sufficient value on the good that now exists to want it to continue to exist.

It surely is sensible to want that. To want it in any case; for itself. Still more to want it in view of what will replace it if we let it go.

Conclusion

Here we have in these old towns of ours many pleasant qualities. Variety, liveliness, comeliness; most times a kind of modest unselfconscious charm and gaiety, frequently striking architectural quality, sometimes even beauty itself. There is almost always interesting and varied townscape; almost always individuality and an attractive settled character, a single whole character (in the High Streets and adjoining streets at least) to which most things subscribe. All these qualities and attributes which our old towns *now have* are enormously worth possessing. Even if we could be sure that ultimately, in the distant future, the now-disruptive buildings would have become so general as to constitute a new and in their own form an equally attractive character, the present character would still be worth maintaining. For the inescapable thing is that in the meanwhile the piecemeal rebuilding must inevitably be disruptive; that over the long course of its continuance to its completion it *must* produce a kind of architectural schizophrenia that would be extremely painful to have to witness and to live with. For a quick wholesale rebuilding such as would avoid it is impossible. As was said earlier on, there is neither the money nor the labour to do it; and even if there were, the chaotic social disturbance that would result would be intolerable. These old towns are with us here and now, and must inevitably be with us, even if in an emasculated form, for a long time to come. The only rational thing, then, in view both of their present attractive character and of the consequences of casually changing it, is to conserve them in that character.

To do that does not mean wholesale preservation. Nor does it mean the limitation of architectural innovations or the imitation of past forms in such rebuilding as may take place. It merely means that in these places new buildings should subscribe to the prevailing character of the street, the building complex, to which they are being added. Their design may be of a new kind. There need not, and should not be, any prohibition against that. But new as they may be, they can and should subscribe to the character of their surroundings instead of being disruptive of it. For street buildings that mainly means subscribing to the existing rhythm of the street. For freer-standing buildings it means subscribing to the rhythm of the general skyline of the town.

And, of course, in all this it is the central parts of the older towns of settled character that are mainly in mind. The principle of street-rhythm cannot properly be wholly ignored even in large cities and the towns (chiefly the industrial towns) of a different character, though the considerations that have been advanced against the building of high towers apply there too. But conservation of existing character is not so necessary there – may even be undesirable. And in the new towns that are being built no considerations of existing disciplines arise. There all things new can be done in their own right. But here in these older towns that we have been concerned with there are qualities that ought to be respected if we have any claim to be sensible and civilized; and which, being respected, should be maintained, not only for ourselves but for future generations to enjoy.

That is all that we have tried to establish here – that present good should be maintained and extended; and that there are ways of appreciating and enjoying it in a wider sense than is generally realized.

INDEX

Index